Calm Before the Exam

Strategies to Ease Test Anxiety

Impress Academics

Table of Contents

Introduction

Understanding and Overcoming Test Anxiety

Sarah's heart raced as she entered the exam hall, a sensation many of us are familiar with. Her palms became sweaty, and her mind seemed to fog over despite all her hours of diligent preparation. It's a scenario that countless students face—sitting down to take an important test only to be overwhelmed by anxiety. These feelings are not just jitters; they can deeply impact one's ability to recall information and think clearly during exams, turning what should be a demonstration of knowledge into an ordeal.

Test anxiety is a pervasive issue affecting a significant portion of students at all academic levels. Research from the American Test Anxieties Association indicates that nearly one-third of students experience considerable test-related stress. This anxiety isn't merely a fleeting nervousness; it's a condition that can trigger physical symptoms like rapid heartbeat, sweating, and shortness of breath. Coupled with psychological symptoms such as racing thoughts and intense fear of failure, test anxiety can create a perfect storm that hampers academic performance. Studies have shown that unmanaged anxiety leads to lower grades, reduced self-confidence, and diminished academic achievement.

This chapter will delve into understanding test anxiety and explore its far-reaching impacts on students' lives. It will examine how anxiety affects both the mind and body, disrupting cognitive functions critical for test-taking. We will discuss evidence-based strategies to manage these symptoms, including cognitive-behavioral techniques, mindfulness practices, and relaxation exercises. By implementing these methods, students can learn to approach exams with a calmer, more focused mindset, better showcasing their true abilities and breaking free from the cycle of anxiety and poor performance.

Engaging Hook and Highlighting the Problem

As Sarah sat down in the exam hall, her palms began to sweat, and she felt a familiar wave of panic wash over her. Her heart was pounding so loudly that she wondered if others could hear it. The words on the test paper blurred together, and her mind raced uncontrollably. She had studied hard for this exam, but now her thoughts were a chaotic mess. Despite all her preparation, Sarah's performance suffered significantly due to overwhelming test anxiety.

Sarah's experience is not unique. Test anxiety is an insidious issue affecting students at all academic levels. A study from the American Test Anxieties Association reveals that approximately 16-20% of students have high test anxiety, while another 18% are moderately test-anxious. This means nearly a third of students experience significant stress during exams, which can drastically impact their academic performance.

Well-documented studies have consistently shown that unmanaged test anxiety can lead to lower grades and diminished academic achievement. A seminal article published in the Journal of Educational Psychology underscores this, revealing that students with high levels of test anxiety perform worse on assessments compared to their less anxious peers. This pervasive issue highlights the urgent need for effective strategies to manage test anxiety, ensuring that students can demonstrate their true capabilities.

The issue of test anxiety is widespread, with profound implications for students' academic performance, well-being, and self-confidence. It's more than just a fleeting feeling of nervousness; it's a debilitating condition that can substantially hinder performance. When faced with tests, students often experience a cascade of physiological symptoms such as rapid heartbeat, excessive sweating, and shortness of breath. These physical manifestations are coupled with psychological symptoms like racing thoughts, intense fear of failure, and difficulty concentrating.

These symptoms aren't just uncomfortable; they directly interfere with cognitive functions critical for test-taking. For instance, anxiety can impair memory recall, making it difficult for students to retrieve information they've studied. It can also cloud decision-making processes, leading to second-guessing and mistakes. This combination of factors results in a detrimental cycle where anxiety begets poor performance, which in turn increases anxiety.

Moreover, the long-term consequences of unaddressed test anxiety are concerning. Students may find their academic potential stunted, as repeated poor performances erode their confidence and motivation. Over time, this can spiral into a decrease in self-esteem and an increase in overall stress levels, affecting not just academic life but personal and professional domains as well.

The physiological responses to test anxiety can often be triggered by the body's fight-or-flight response, an automatic reaction to perceived threats. While this response might have been essential for early humans facing immediate dangers, it's far less helpful when the "threat" is a test paper. Rapid heartbeat and sweating are signs that the body is preparing for a quick getaway or a battle, neither of which are beneficial in a testing environment.

Understanding these reactions is crucial for developing strategies to mitigate them. Cognitive-behavioral techniques, mindfulness practices, and relaxation exercises can help students manage their physiological and psychological responses. By addressing the underlying causes of anxiety, students can learn to approach exams with a calmer mindset, better equipping them to perform to the best of their abilities.

Cognitive-behavioral therapy (CBT) has been particularly effective in helping students manage test anxiety. CBT focuses on changing negative thought patterns that contribute to anxiety. For example, a student who believes they will fail no matter how much they study can reframe this thought to recognize their efforts and acknowledge past successes. This shift in mindset can reduce anxiety and improve self-confidence.

Additionally, mindfulness practices, such as meditation and deep-breathing exercises, can help students stay grounded and focused. These practices teach students to remain present in the moment, reducing the tendency to ruminate on past failures or future worries. Over time, mindfulness can cultivate a sense of inner calm, making it easier to manage test-related stress.

Relaxation techniques like progressive muscle relaxation or guided imagery can also be beneficial. These methods involve consciously relaxing different muscle groups or visualizing calming scenes to reduce physical tension. Regular practice of these techniques can help students develop a toolkit of strategies to employ during stressful situations, including exams.

The importance of creating a supportive environment cannot be overstated. Educational institutions and educators play a pivotal role in addressing test anxiety. Simple changes, such as providing a less stressful testing environment and offering resources for anxiety management, can make a significant difference. Encouraging a growth mindset, where students see challenges as opportunities for learning rather than threats, can also foster resilience against anxiety.

It's also vital for students to practice self-care, especially during exam periods. Adequate sleep, proper nutrition, regular exercise, and breaks between study sessions can significantly impact stress levels and overall well-being. When students take care of their bodies, they are better equipped to handle the mental demands of academics.

As we consider the landscape of test anxiety, it's clear that a multifaceted approach is necessary. Combining practical strategies at both the individual and institutional levels can create an environment where students thrive academically and personally. Policies should emphasize the importance of mental health and establish support systems that guide students toward effective strategies for managing anxiety.

In conclusion, test anxiety is a complex issue with far-reaching effects on students' academic success and personal well-being. By understanding its root causes and symptoms, we can begin to implement evidence-based strategies to tackle it. From cognitive-behavioral techniques and mindfulness practices to supportive educational environments and robust self-care routines, there are numerous ways to empower students to overcome test anxiety. Through these concerted efforts, we can ensure that students not only succeed in their exams but also build resilience and confidence for the future.

Addressing Reader's Pain Points and Building Trust

It is no secret that test anxiety can feel overwhelming. If you've ever found yourself in the midst of an exam, heart racing and mind going blank, you are not alone. Many students share this experience. Feeling powerless, trapped in a cycle of worry, is more common than we often realize. It's important to acknowledge these feelings because they are valid and widely experienced.

Imagine walking into a room, prepared for a test you've studied hard for, only to be greeted by a wave of nerves strong enough to wash away days, weeks, or even months of preparation. This emotional response isn't just frustrating; it can feel like a betrayal by your own body and mind. You may start doubting your capabilities, questioning your worth, and wondering if you'll ever improve.

Addressing test anxiety is crucial because it affects both your emotional well-being and academic performance. It's easy to get caught in a negative feedback loop where anxiety begets poor performance, which in turn increases anxiety. Breaking out of this cycle requires understanding and strategies that are backed by research and practical application.

It's reassuring to note that effective strategies do exist. By recognizing common symptoms and using evidence-based approaches, you can manage your anxiety levels, perform better academically, and regain confidence in your abilities. This book aims to serve as your guide, offering insight from experts who have dedicated their careers to studying and alleviating test anxiety.

To increase credibility, it's worth mentioning my background in education and psychology. Over years of working with students and professionals alike, I've witnessed firsthand how debilitating test anxiety can be. My approach isn't just theoretical; it's firmly rooted in empirical evidence and real-world success stories. Numerous research studies highlight techniques that effectively reduce test anxiety, such as cognitive-behavioral strategies, mindfulness practices, and relaxation techniques.

For instance, a study from the Journal of Educational Psychology found that students who engaged in regular mindfulness exercises reported significantly lower anxiety levels and improved test performance. This kind of data reinforces the value of incorporating structured, evidence-based practices into your daily routine. Moreover, testimonials from students who've transformed their academic trajectories thanks to these strategies demonstrate their practicality and effectiveness.

One student, Jane, came to me during her final semester, paralyzed by the fear of exams. She had always been a diligent student but struggled immensely when it came to tests. Through implementing specific anxiety-reduction techniques discussed in this book, she learned to control her breathing, redirect her thoughts, and enter exams with a newfound sense of calmness. Her grades improved dramatically, and she graduated with honors— a testament to the power of effective strategies.

Understanding test anxiety means recognizing its physiological and psychological dimensions. It's not just 'all in your head.' When you're anxious, your body's stress response kicks in, leading to rapid heartbeat, sweating, and sometimes, even shortness of breath. These physical symptoms can exacerbate mental ones, like racing thoughts and a pervasive fear of failure. It's essential to understand this interplay to address both the mind and body in managing test anxiety.

Cognitive functions can also be impaired by test anxiety. During heightened states of anxiety, your brain's ability to recall information diminishes. The pressure causes a sort of mental block, making it harder to retrieve memories or think clearly. This can significantly affect your performance, no matter how well you know the material. Solutions, therefore, must target improving clarity of thought and memory recall under stress.

Long-term consequences of unaddressed test anxiety are profound. Chronic anxiety can lead to reduced academic potential, decreased self-esteem, and heightened overall stress levels. For adult learners and professionals, this can translate into stunted career growth and missed opportunities. Addressing these challenges head-on is vital for unlocking one's full potential.

The good news is that there are actionable steps you can take to alleviate test anxiety:

- First, practice mindfulness and relaxation techniques regularly. Activities such as deep breathing exercises, progressive muscle relaxation, and guided imagery can help lower your body's stress response.

- Second, implement cognitive-behavioral strategies to change negative thought patterns. Challenge irrational fears about failure and replace them with positive affirmations and realistic appraisals of your abilities.

- Third, establish a consistent study routine that incorporates breaks and rewards. Breaking study sessions into manageable chunks, followed by periods of rest, prevents burnout and enhances retention.

- Fourth, simulate testing conditions during your study sessions. Practice under timed circumstances and in environments similar to where you'll be taking the test. This helps familiarize your brain with the experience, reducing surprise and anxiety on the actual test day.

These techniques don't require major lifestyle changes; rather, they integrate seamlessly into your existing routines. Test anxiety isn't an insurmountable barrier; it's a challenge that, once understood and managed, can become a source of personal strength and resilience.

In closing, remember that you're not alone in facing test anxiety, and many before you have successfully navigated this path. With the right strategies and a willingness to engage with these approaches, you too can transform your experience. Let this book be a resource and companion in your journey towards overcoming test anxiety, improving your academic performance, and building the confidence you need to succeed.

Through the combined efforts of educators, psychologists, and countless students' experiences, we've accumulated knowledge and techniques that genuinely work. Together, armed with evidence-based practices, you can confront test anxiety head-on and emerge not just unscathed, but stronger and more capable than ever before.

Setting the Stage for Success

In this chapter, we delved into the pervasive issue of test anxiety, particularly its profound impact on students' academic performance and well-being. We began by sharing Sarah's experience, a scenario that resonates with many, illustrating how test anxiety can undermine even the best-prepared individual's efforts. The statistics emphasize the scale of this problem, showing that nearly a third of students grapple with significant test-related stress.

Test anxiety manifests in both physiological and psychological symptoms, which can severely disrupt cognitive functions vital for exam success. This debilitating condition doesn't just affect academic performance; it also erodes self-confidence and long-term motivation, potentially impacting personal and professional growth in the future. Recognizing these symptoms is the first step towards managing them effectively.

As we explored, unmanaged test anxiety triggers a fight-or-flight response that is counterproductive in an exam setting. By understanding these reactions, one can employ strategies to mitigate them. Cognitive-behavioral techniques, mindfulness practices, and relaxation exercises have shown immense potential in helping students manage their anxiety. These approaches not only address the symptoms but also tackle the underlying thought patterns contributing to the anxiety.

Our discussion underscored the importance of a supportive environment provided by educational institutions and educators. Simple adjustments, such as creating less stressful testing conditions and promoting a growth mindset, can significantly impact students' ability to handle anxiety. Similarly, self-care routines, including adequate sleep, nutrition, and exercise, play a crucial role in preparing the mind and body to face academic challenges.

Understanding test anxiety and tackling its root causes enables students to perform to their true potential. The strategies highlighted in this chapter, ranging from cognitive-behavioral techniques to mindfulness practices, offer practical tools to manage anxiety effectively. These methods are not mere academic theories but real-world solutions grounded in empirical evidence and proven success stories.

Looking ahead, it's crucial to acknowledge that addressing test anxiety requires a multifaceted approach, combining individual efforts with institutional support. By prioritizing mental health and implementing robust support systems, we can create an environment where students thrive academically and personally. As you continue your journey, consider integrating these strategies into your routine. Embrace the process, build resilience, and transform anxiety into an opportunity for growth and strength.

Chapter 1

Test Anxiety: Psychological Effects and Impact on Exam Performance

Test anxiety is a common experience that can significantly impact an individual's ability to perform well on exams. For many adult students and professionals, the mere thought of taking a test can trigger a cascade of physical, emotional, and cognitive symptoms that disrupt their capacity to recall information and solve problems effectively. This phenomenon is not limited to any one demographic or field but spans across various age groups and disciplines. Understanding the intricate dynamics of test anxiety is essential for developing strategies to manage it and improve exam performance.

Unlike typical pre-exam stress, which can serve as a motivating force, test anxiety often manifests in more severe and debilitating ways. Imagine sitting in an exam room with beads of sweat forming on your forehead, your heart racing, and your mind going blank despite extensive preparation. These are some of the physical symptoms many face when dealing with test anxiety. Emotionally, individuals may experience feelings of dread, panic, or a sense of impending doom. Cognitively, they might struggle with racing thoughts, difficulty concentrating, or completely blanking out during an exam. Such experiences create a vicious cycle where anxiety begets poor performance, which in turn heightens future anxiety, thus perpetuating the problem.

In this chapter, we will delve into the psychological effects of test anxiety and how they impact exam performance. We will explore the differences between normal exam stress and test anxiety, identify common symptoms, and examine the factors contributing to this condition. Additionally, we will outline practical strategies and coping mechanisms designed to help you navigate these challenges effectively. By gaining a comprehensive understanding of test anxiety and its multifaceted impacts, you will be better equipped to manage your stress levels and enhance your academic or professional performance during exams.

Understanding the Difference Between Normal Exam Stress and Test Anxiety

Understanding the difference between normal exam stress and test anxiety is crucial for anyone aiming to manage their mental well-being effectively during exams. Test anxiety involves a heightened level of fear or worry that goes beyond typical nervousness before exams. It's important to acknowledge that feeling anxious before an exam is completely normal and can often be motivating. However, when this anxiety intensifies to the point where it disrupts your ability to perform, it crosses into the territory of test anxiety.

Recognizing the physical and emotional symptoms that differentiate test anxiety from regular exam stress is a significant step in addressing the issue. Physical symptoms of test anxiety can include sweating, rapid heartbeat, headaches, and even gastrointestinal issues. On the emotional side, you might experience excessive worry, feelings of dread, or an overwhelming urge to escape the situation.

Here is what you can do in order to identify the symptoms:

- Pay attention to your body's signals as you approach the exam date.
- Reflect on whether your worries are manageable or if they become overarching concerns that overshadow other thoughts.
- Seek feedback from friends or family who may notice changes in your behavior or mood as the exam approaches.

The strategies to identify when exam stress crosses the threshold into debilitating test anxiety are vital for timely intervention. Ask yourself whether your anxiety impacts your daily routines or prevents you from studying effectively. If you find yourself unable to concentrate on your revision, procrastinating excessively, or experiencing panic attacks, it's likely that your exam stress has escalated into test anxiety.

To navigate this effectively:

- Maintain a diary to track your stress levels and identify patterns.
- Consult with a mental health professional who can provide diagnostic clarity and actionable advice.
- Engage in open conversations with peers, mentors, or instructors to gain perspective and support.

Techniques to distinguish between adaptive and maladaptive anxiety responses to exams can empower you to turn potentially harmful stress into productive energy. Adaptive anxiety may heighten alertness and focus, enhancing performance. On the contrary, maladaptive anxiety can lead to avoidance behaviors, lack of concentration, and ultimately poor exam performance.

Consider these steps to make that distinction:

- Evaluate how your anxiety influences your study habits: Are you more disciplined, or do you find yourself avoiding study sessions?
- Observe the outcomes of your anxiety: Does it help you organize better, or does it leave you feeling paralyzed?
- Create a clear plan for exam preparation: Break down your study material into manageable chunks and set realistic goals to keep your anxiety within productive bounds.

By understanding the distinction between normal exam stress and test anxiety, readers can recognize and address concerning levels of anxiety effectively. Awareness is the first step toward managing any form of stress or anxiety. Armed with this knowledge, you'll be better equipped to identify when extra support or different coping strategies are needed.

In essence, recognizing test anxiety isn't about eliminating all stress—some level of stress is natural and can be functional. It's about ensuring that anxiety serves as a catalyst rather than a hindrance to your success. By being attuned to both your physical and emotional responses, you can develop personalized strategies that draw on your strengths and align with your needs.

Identifying Common Symptoms of Test Anxiety

Understanding and managing test anxiety is paramount for adult students and professionals seeking to enhance their exam performance. By identifying the common symptoms of test anxiety, individuals can better grasp their own experiences and seek appropriate support and coping strategies. Let's delve into the physical, cognitive, emotional, and behavioral manifestations of test anxiety.

One prominent set of symptoms associated with test anxiety is physical in nature. These can be significantly distressing and may include a rapid heartbeat, sweating, and nausea. When you're about to take an exam and you find your heart racing, palms sweating, or stomach churning, it's often a sign that your body's fight-or-flight response has been triggered. This physiological reaction is perfectly normal but can become problematic when it affects your ability to perform well on exams.

Here's what you can do to manage these physical symptoms:

- Practice deep breathing exercises to calm your nervous system.

- Ensure you are well-hydrated and have a balanced diet leading up to the exam.
- Engage in regular physical activity to alleviate stress.
- Incorporate relaxation techniques such as progressive muscle relaxation or yoga into your routine.

The second category of symptoms encompasses cognitive effects. Cognitive symptoms of test anxiety can manifest as racing thoughts, difficulty concentrating, or even blanking out during exams. Imagine sitting down to a test you've studied hard for, only to find that your mind goes completely blank, or you're unable to focus on the questions in front of you. This mental fog can be extremely frustrating and disheartening.

To mitigate cognitive symptoms, consider these strategies:

- Break study materials into smaller, manageable sections to avoid overwhelming yourself.
- Use positive affirmations and visualizations to foster a sense of preparedness and confidence.
- Employ active learning techniques such as summarizing information in your own words or teaching it to someone else.
- Take short breaks during study sessions to allow your brain to rest and reset.

Test anxiety also manifests emotionally, with signs such as feelings of dread, panic, or a sense of impending doom. These emotions can create a vicious cycle wherein the more anxious you feel, the worse your performance, and the worse your performance, the more anxious you become. It's essential to recognize that feeling intense emotions before an exam is not unusual and does not define your abilities or worth.

Managing emotional symptoms involves:

- Acknowledging and naming your emotions rather than suppressing them.
- Engaging in mindfulness meditation to stay grounded and present.
- Connecting with a supportive peer, mentor, or counselor who can offer encouragement and advice.
- Limiting exposure to negative narratives or comparisons with others.

Behavioral manifestations are another critical aspect of test anxiety. Behaviors such as avoidance, procrastination, or perfectionism can sabotage your preparation process and exacerbate anxiety. Avoidance might mean not attending review sessions or neglecting certain subjects altogether because they trigger anxiety. Procrastination often results in last-minute cramming, which is far less effective than consistent, spaced-out study sessions. Perfectionism creates unrealistic standards that heighten anxiety and fear of failure.

Consider these approaches to address behavioral symptoms:

- Establish a realistic study schedule and adhere to it consistently.
- Use tools like planners or apps to keep track of deadlines and progress.
- Reward yourself for small accomplishments to stay motivated.
- Set achievable goals and acknowledge that perfection is not the goal—progress is.

By being aware of the various symptoms of test anxiety, individuals can better identify their own experiences and seek appropriate support and coping strategies. It's important to remember that everyone experiences some degree of anxiety, especially in high-stakes situations like exams. Recognizing the symptoms is the first step toward managing them effectively.

Physical symptoms, like a rapid heartbeat, sweating, and nausea, serve as clear indicators of the body's heightened state of alert. These reactions are deeply rooted in our evolutionary survival mechanisms, designed to prepare us to face threats. However, in the context of a modern exam room, they can be counterproductive. Through deep breathing exercises, maintaining a healthy lifestyle, and incorporating relaxation techniques, you can significantly alleviate these physical manifestations.

On the cognitive front, racing thoughts, difficulty concentrating, and blanking out are common challenges. The brain, under stress, tends to either hyperfocus on the source of anxiety or shut down altogether. Breaking study materials into smaller chunks, using positive affirmations, employing active learning techniques, and taking regular breaks can help keep your mind sharp and focused.

Emotional symptoms—feelings of dread, panic, or doom—can be particularly paralyzing. They feed off each other, creating a feedback loop that increases anxiety levels. Naming your emotions, practicing mindfulness, seeking support from peers or counselors, and avoiding negative self-talk can help break this cycle and foster a more positive outlook.

Behavioral symptoms, including avoidance, procrastination, and perfectionism, often act as coping mechanisms that ultimately undermine success. Creating a realistic study plan, utilizing organizational tools, rewarding incremental progress, and setting achievable goals can redirect these behaviors into more productive pathways.

In sum, understanding the multifaceted nature of test anxiety empowers individuals to tackle it from multiple angles. Whether through physical relaxation techniques, cognitive restructuring, emotional regulation, or behavioral modification, there are numerous strategies available to support those struggling with test anxiety. By adopting a holistic approach that addresses all these dimensions, adult students and professionals can improve their exam performance and reduce anxiety levels significantly.

Every student's journey with test anxiety is unique, and what works for one person may not work for another. Therefore, it's crucial to experiment with different strategies and tailor them to fit your personal needs. Remember, the overarching goal is to create a balanced approach that prioritizes human welfare over economic growth, reflecting a commitment to both individual freedom and social responsibility. Empowering people with the right tools and knowledge to manage their anxiety not only enhances personal performance but also contributes to a healthier, more equitable society.

Exploring the Factors Contributing to Test Anxiety

Internal factors such as negative self-talk, self-doubt, and fear of failure can exacerbate test anxiety. When we allow our inner critic to run rampant, it's akin to having a personal saboteur that undermines our confidence just when we need it the most. Think about those moments when you've found yourself mulling over thoughts like "I'm just not smart enough," or "What if I fail?" This kind of negative self-talk doesn't just arise from nowhere; it's often deeply ingrained through years of habit and experience.

Here is what you can do in order to manage these internal factors:

- Start by recognizing and acknowledging your negative thoughts. Awareness is the first step towards change.

- Challenge these thoughts by asking, "Is this really true? Is there evidence to support this belief?"

- Replace negative statements with realistic, positive affirmations. For example, instead of thinking "I can't do this," try "I've prepared, and I'm capable of doing my best."

Additionally, self-doubt can creep into our minds, especially when previous academic experiences have been less than stellar. One way to combat self-doubt is by setting realistic goals and breaking down study tasks into manageable parts. This can create a sense of achievement at each step, which builds confidence over time. Regularly reminding yourself of your past successes, no matter how small, can also help reframe your mindset toward one of capability and resilience.

Now, let's turn to external factors like pressure from family, peers, or academic expectations. The pressure to meet the high standards set by others—or ones we impose on ourselves—can significantly heighten anxiety levels. Families and friends often mean well, but their expectations can sometimes be burdensome. Suppose you're striving to meet the expectations of a family member who sees success in a certain light. It's crucial to have open conversations about your own goals and limits.

Here is how you can navigate these external pressures effectively:

- Communicate openly with family and peers about your needs and boundaries. Assertiveness is key here.

- Seek social support where you feel understood and accepted. Surrounding yourself with supportive people can alleviate anxiety.

- Set and prioritize your own goals. Understanding what you want out of your education can reduce the weight of others' expectations.

External academic pressures, particularly those stemming from competitive environments, can also add layers to your stress. Schools and universities often cultivate competitive atmospheres that can make even the most confident students feel overwhelmed. A practical approach to manage this is by focusing on personal improvement rather than competing against others. Celebrate your progress and understand that everyone has their unique journey.

Examining the impact of past negative experiences with exams or performance-related trauma can shed light on why anxiety persists today. Traumatic experiences, like failing an important exam or experiencing severe stress during a crucial testing moment, leave lasting impressions. These experiences can cause conditioned responses where the mere thought of upcoming exams triggers anxiety. To address these reactions, it can be helpful to reflect on those past events in a safe and structured way. Techniques such as journaling about your experiences or discussing them with a counselor can help desensitize these fears over time. Engaging in practices like mindfulness and relaxation exercises can also lessen anxiety by calming the mind and body before an exam.

Finally, let's delve into understanding how personal beliefs about intelligence, worth, and success influence test anxiety levels. Many of us carry deep-seated beliefs about our capabilities and self-worth tied directly to our academic achievements. If you believe that intelligence is fixed and unchangeable, this can lead to a fear of failure, as any setback might seem like a reflection of your intrinsic worth. Conversely, adopting a growth mindset—the belief that abilities can improve through effort and perseverance—can reduce anxiety. With a growth mindset, mistakes are seen as opportunities to learn rather than as definitive judgments of your abilities.

These beliefs don't change overnight, but incremental shifts in thinking can make a significant difference. For instance, start by framing challenges as learning opportunities. Instead of saying, "I'm bad at math," you might say, "Math is challenging for me, but with practice, I can improve." It's essential to explore these deeply held beliefs and understand how they shape your reactions to academic stressors.

By recognizing the multifaceted nature of factors contributing to test anxiety, individuals can address both internal and external triggers to reduce anxiety levels effectively. This holistic understanding empowers you to tackle anxiety from multiple angles. You're not just dealing with stress in the present moment but addressing its root causes, whether they're internal voices critiquing your every move, external pressures from those around you, past experiences that haunt you, or deeply held beliefs about your worth and intelligence.

In conclusion, tackling test anxiety requires a comprehensive approach that acknowledges and addresses the diverse elements at play. It's not just about studying harder or longer; it's about cultivating a healthier relationship with yourself, your environment, and your past experiences. Remember, test anxiety doesn't define you. With awareness, effort, and the right strategies, it's entirely possible to mitigate its effects and perform at your best when it counts.

Understanding the Effects of Test Anxiety on Cognitive Functions

Test anxiety is a multifaceted issue that affects more than just the emotional state of individuals; it has far-reaching impacts on our cognitive functions. Let's delve into how this phenomenon plays out and how it can significantly affect exam performance.

Firstly, it's critical to understand that test anxiety can severely impair memory retrieval, attention span, and information processing speed during exams. When anxiety levels peak, the brain's ability to access stored information becomes compromised. Think of your brain as a well-organized file cabinet. Under normal circumstances, you can easily find the file you need. However, under stress, it's as if someone scattered those files all over the floor. The process of sifting through this mess takes time and often results in not finding the information at all. Research supports this by showing that anxiety diverts mental resources away from the task at hand, making it difficult to focus and retrieve information effectively.

Moreover, test anxiety doesn't just pop up randomly; it has longer-term consequences. Chronic test anxiety may lead to consistent academic underperformance, lower grades, and decreased confidence in one's abilities. Imagine facing a hurdle race every time you enter an exam room, knowing there's a high likelihood you'll trip. It's no wonder then that students with chronic test anxiety often see a pattern of diminished academic achievement. This repetitive cycle of anxiety and underachievement can erode self-esteem over time, making it harder for individuals to motivate themselves to prepare adequately for future exams.

Shifting gears a bit, it's essential to discuss how our bodies react physiologically to test anxiety. One of the most immediate responses to anxiety is the release of stress hormones like cortisol and adrenaline. These hormones are designed to prepare us for a "fight or flight" response, which, while useful in life-threatening situations, isn't particularly helpful in a quiet exam room. Elevated levels of these hormones can disrupt the brain regions responsible for higher-order thinking and problem-solving. Essentially, when your body goes into fight-or-flight mode, it prioritizes basic survival instincts over complex thought processes.

Now, let's explore the link between heightened anxiety levels and reduced problem-solving skills or critical thinking abilities. When you're anxious, your brain's prefrontal cortex, which is responsible for logical thinking and decision-making, doesn't function as efficiently. Instead, the amygdala, which handles emotional responses, takes over. This shift in brain activity means that tasks requiring critical thinking and intricate problem-solving become exceedingly challenging. Studies have shown that anxious individuals often resort to more superficial processing strategies, such as rote memorization, rather than deep learning methods. This surface-level engagement further hampers their performance on tasks that require a more nuanced understanding of concepts or problems.

So, what does this mean for those struggling with test anxiety? By understanding how it impacts cognitive functions, individuals can adopt targeted strategies to manage anxiety and optimize exam performance. While each person's experience with anxiety is unique, a common starting point is recognizing the importance of mental and physical preparation. Techniques such as mindfulness meditation, controlled breathing exercises, and regular physical activity can help regulate stress responses and improve overall mental resilience. Additionally, breaking study material into smaller, manageable sections and using active learning techniques—such as teaching the material to someone else or applying concepts to real-world scenarios—can aid in deeper comprehension and retention of information.

In summary, test anxiety is more than just a case of nerves; it fundamentally impacts our cognitive abilities in several ways. It hampers memory retrieval, narrows attention spans, and slows down information processing speeds. Over time, chronic anxiety can lead to poor academic performance and diminished self-confidence. Physiologically, the release of stress hormones further disrupts cognitive functions, hindering problem-solving and critical thinking abilities. By recognizing and addressing these impacts, individuals can employ effective strategies to mitigate test anxiety and enhance their exam performance. Understanding the intricate relationship between anxiety and cognition offers a pathway toward better academic outcomes and increased confidence in one's abilities.

It's important to approach this topic with empathy and evidence-based solutions. Anxiety doesn't discriminate; it can affect anyone, regardless of age, background, or academic prowess. Recognizing the signs of test anxiety early on and taking proactive steps to manage it can make a world of difference. Consider incorporating relaxation techniques into your daily routine, seeking support from peers or professionals, and, importantly, maintaining a balanced lifestyle that prioritizes both mental and physical health.

Ultimately, the goal is to foster an environment where students feel empowered rather than paralyzed by their anxieties. By adopting a comprehensive approach that encompasses both individual strategies and systemic changes—such as promoting mental health awareness in educational institutions—we can create a more supportive atmosphere for all learners. After all, education should be a journey of discovery and growth, not a constant battle against anxiety.

Therefore, let's continue to advocate for a balanced perspective that recognizes the importance of both personal responsibility and societal support. Only through a collaborative effort, rooted in empirical evidence and guided by empathy, can we hope to address the pervasive issue of test anxiety and its impact on academic performance.

Managing Test Anxiety for Optimal Exam Performance

Understanding the psychological effects of test anxiety and its impact on exam performance requires a holistic perspective. Throughout this chapter, we have examined the defining characteristics of normal exam stress versus test anxiety, identified common symptoms, explored contributing factors, and delved into the cognitive impacts.

Recognizing the distinction between typical exam stress and debilitating test anxiety is pivotal. Normal stress can motivate and focus individuals, while excessive anxiety can disrupt physical health, emotional balance, and cognitive functions. By identifying symptoms such as rapid heartbeat, racing thoughts, feelings of doom, and avoidance behaviors, one can take proactive steps to manage stress levels effectively.

Reflecting on internal and external contributors to anxiety brings us closer to understanding its root causes. Negative self-talk, self-doubt, and fear of failure often fuel test anxiety internally, while external pressures from family, peers, and academic environments compound the issue. Addressing these factors with strategies like challenging negative thoughts, setting realistic goals, and seeking supportive networks can mitigate their adverse effects.

Exploring the cognitive ramifications reveals how anxiety hampers memory retrieval, concentration, and problem-solving abilities. Elevated stress hormones divert mental resources away from the task at hand, making it harder to perform well during exams. Understanding this relationship highlights the importance of adopting physical and mental preparation techniques, such as mindfulness meditation and active learning strategies, to enhance focus and retention.

For readers, the implications are clear: managing test anxiety is not solely about academic performance but also about overall mental well-being. Unchecked anxiety can lead to chronic underperformance, lowered self-esteem, and continuous stress cycles that affect other areas of life.

On a broader scale, addressing test anxiety comprehensively contributes to a healthier educational environment. Educational institutions must prioritize mental health awareness and provide support systems that empower individuals to navigate academic challenges successfully. This approach benefits not just individual students but the community as a whole, promoting a culture of balanced achievement and well-being.

The journey to overcoming test anxiety involves recognizing symptoms, understanding underlying factors, and implementing multifaceted strategies for management. As you continue on this path, remember that progress, not perfection, is the goal. Your unique experience with test anxiety can become an opportunity for growth and resilience. Keep exploring, reflecting, and adapting, and you'll find that anxiety can be managed, enabling you to perform at your best.

Chapter 2

Psychological Techniques for Overcoming Test Anxiety

Imagine sitting in an exam room, the silence punctuated only by the ticking clock and the rustling of papers. Your heart races, palms sweat, and an overwhelming sense of dread washes over you. This scenario is all too familiar for many students who experience test anxiety. But what if there were concrete techniques that could help transform this nerve-wracking experience into one of calm focus? Understanding how cognitive-behavioral strategies can alleviate test anxiety might be the key to unlocking your academic potential.

Test anxiety often stems from deeply rooted irrational beliefs and negative thoughts. These thoughts, such as "I am bound to fail" or "I am not smart enough," create a mental barrier that can hinder performance. For instance, a student convinced they will fail may struggle with confidence and underperform, not due to lack of knowledge but because of their mindset. Similarly, the thought "I'm not good enough" can sabotage even the most well-prepared individual. These beliefs are rarely grounded in reality and instead reflect distorted perceptions. Challenging these assumptions by examining past successes and gathering evidence contrary to these thoughts is a crucial step toward managing anxiety.

This chapter delves into practical cognitive-behavioral strategies designed to reframe negative thoughts and reduce test anxiety. It begins with identifying and challenging irrational beliefs, a foundational exercise in recognizing and debunking false narratives that feed anxiety. The discussion then moves on to techniques for replacing these irrational thoughts with rational, balanced perspectives, thereby fostering a more empowered outlook. Additionally, the chapter highlights the importance of self-compassion and how treating oneself kindly during stressful periods can significantly reduce anxiety levels. By the end of this chapter, you will be equipped with actionable strategies to approach exams with greater confidence and composure, transforming your academic experiences from daunting to manageable.

Identifying and Challenging Irrational Beliefs

Let's take a moment to understand test anxiety and how cognitive-behavioral strategies can help address this issue. We all know that exams are a significant source of stress, but it's essential to recognize what's happening beneath the surface. Sometimes, it's not the exam itself causing the problem but rather our thoughts about it. By identifying and challenging these irrational beliefs, we can shift our mindset toward more positive thinking.

One common negative belief related to exams is the fear of failure, such as "I will fail." This thought alone can be paralyzing and lead to a self-fulfilling prophecy where the expectation of failure contributes to poor performance. Another prevalent belief is feeling inadequate: "I'm not smart enough." It's beneficial to challenge these thoughts by examining evidence contrary to them. For instance, consider your past successes. Have you succeeded in other tests or academic pursuits before? Reflecting on these achievements provides concrete proof that these negative beliefs may not be accurate.

Here is what you can do to challenge these irrational beliefs:

- Start by writing down the negative thoughts you have about exams.

- Next, gather evidence that challenges these thoughts. Look for instances when you performed well or received positive feedback.
- Ask yourself if the negative belief is based on facts or just an assumption.
- Compare the negative thought with the facts and see if it holds up.

The next step involves replacing those irrational thoughts with rational and balanced perspectives. It's vital to acknowledge your capabilities and past successes. When the thought "I will fail" arises, counter it with "I have prepared thoroughly, and I have succeeded before." Acting on these rational perspectives enables you to build confidence over time.

To replace irrational thoughts effectively, try these steps:

- First, identify the irrational thought you want to change.
- Then, think of a rational thought that counters it.
- Every time the irrational thought pops into your mind, consciously replace it with the rational one.
- Practice this regularly to make it a habit.

Practicing self-compassion and kindness towards oneself is another crucial aspect. It's important to recognize that everyone has moments of doubt and making errors is part of the learning process. When faced with challenging beliefs, it helps to treat yourself as you would a good friend. Offer yourself words of encouragement and understanding instead of harsh criticism. This approach fosters a sense of acceptance and reduces anxiety. Remember, being kind to yourself isn't about avoiding responsibility; it's about giving yourself the support needed to overcome difficulties.

Using cognitive-behavioral techniques like cognitive restructuring can also significantly impact how you perceive exams. Cognitive restructuring involves changing the way you think about something in order to change how you feel about it. By reframing negative beliefs into more empowering and optimistic statements, you can alter both your thoughts and emotions.

Here's how you can apply cognitive restructuring:

- Identify the negative thought that causes anxiety.
- Challenge the thought by asking questions like, "Is this thought helpful?" or "What evidence do I have that contradicts this thought?"
- Develop a balanced thought that is more realistic and less distressing.
- Write down the balanced thought and remind yourself of it regularly.

For example, if your negative belief is "I'm not smart enough," ask yourself whether there is evidence supporting this claim. You might realize that your grades have generally been good or that you've learned complex topics before. A balanced perspective could be, "I may find some subjects challenging, but I have the ability to learn and improve."

Recognizing and disputing irrational beliefs can profoundly affect how you approach exams. It allows you to reframe your thoughts, enhancing self-confidence and reducing anxiety. When negative thoughts creep in, challenging them with evidence and replacing them with balanced perspectives helps reinforce a healthier way of thinking. Practicing self-compassion ensures you don't fall into the trap of self-criticism, which only exacerbates anxiety. And cognitive restructuring provides the tools to transform your mindset from one of defeat to one of empowerment.

By adopting these strategies, you're taking control of your thought processes. You're actively choosing not to let irrational fears dictate your actions. Instead, you're focusing on what's within your power: preparation, knowledge, and a positive mindset. Remember, exams are just one moment in time—they don't define your worth or intelligence. Your genuine effort, resilience, and ability to adapt are far more telling of your potential and capability.

It's also worth noting that these skills and strategies extend beyond academic exams. They are applicable in various stressful situations, whether it's a job interview, a presentation, or any high-pressure scenario. The ability to manage your thoughts and maintain a positive outlook is invaluable across different aspects of life.

Incorporating these cognitive-behavioral strategies won't happen overnight. It requires consistent practice and patience. But the investment in learning and applying these techniques is well worth it. Not only will they help reduce test anxiety, but they'll also contribute to overall mental well-being. As you continue practicing these methods, you'll likely notice a decrease in anxiety levels and an increase in self-confidence and performance.

Finally, remember that it's okay to seek additional support if you need it. Speaking with a therapist or counselor trained in cognitive-behavioral therapy can provide further guidance tailored to your specific needs. You don't have to navigate this journey alone—there are resources and people ready to help you succeed.

In summary, by identifying and challenging irrational beliefs, replacing them with rational thoughts, practicing self-compassion, and utilizing cognitive restructuring, you can effectively reframe your thoughts and reduce anxiety. These strategies empower you to approach exams—and other stressful situations—with a clearer, more confident mindset. Keep practicing, stay patient, and reach out for support when necessary. You've got this.

Implementing Positive Self-Talk and Affirmations

When it comes to preparing for exams, the power of positive self-talk and affirmations can't be overstated. This isn't just about being overly optimistic; it's about harnessing practical tools to manage anxiety and build confidence.

Developing a list of positive affirmations specific to exam preparation is a foundational step. These affirmations might include statements like "I am well-prepared and capable of performing to the best of my abilities." The purpose here is to create a mental script that reinforces your readiness and competence.

Here is what you can do in order to achieve the goal:

- Start by identifying areas where you feel anxious or doubtful.
- Formulate affirmations that directly counter those negative thoughts. For instance, if you're worried about forgetting material, an affirmation could be: "I remember everything I study."
- Write these affirmations down in a notebook or on flashcards.
- Repeat them daily, ideally in the morning and before studying sessions.

This exercise doesn't take much time, but it has the potential to significantly alter your mindset. When you continuously repeat positive affirmations, you're effectively rewiring your brain to focus on success rather than failure.

Next, let's talk about practicing self-talk techniques. It's essential to develop a habit of encouraging yourself, especially when facing challenges or setbacks during exams. This is not just wishful thinking; it's about building resilience and fostering a positive attitude.

Here is what you can do in order to practice self-talk techniques:

- Pay attention to your inner dialogue. Are you often harsh and critical? If so, make a conscious effort to change this.
- Replace negative self-talk with supportive and motivating messages. Instead of saying "I'll never get this right," try "I can figure this out if I keep trying."
- Encourage yourself as you would a friend who is struggling. Use phrases that promote self-belief and perseverance.

- Keep a journal of your self-talk experiences. Note when you successfully shift your thoughts from negative to positive. Over time, this will become second nature.

Visualization techniques are another powerful tool to mentally rehearse positive outcomes. Visualization leverages the brain's ability to simulate experiences, helping you to 'see' success before it happens.

Here is how to effectively use visualization techniques:

- Find a quiet place free from distractions. Close your eyes and take a few deep breaths to relax.

- Visualize yourself confidently walking into the exam room. Picture yourself answering questions smoothly and correctly. See yourself completing the exam and feeling satisfied with your performance.

- Focus on the details. What does the room look like? How do you feel sitting at your desk? Engaging all your senses makes the visualization more impactful.

- Repeat this visualization regularly, such as once a day during your study routine. The more vivid and consistent the images, the stronger the positive reinforcement.

Visualizing a successful outcome helps reduce anxiety by familiarizing your brain with the process of achieving your goals. It transforms exam preparation from a daunting task into a series of manageable steps leading to a confident finish.

Engage in regular affirmations and self-talk practices to build a resilient mindset and counteract negative self-perceptions. This practice isn't limited to the moments before or during an exam. Make it a part of your daily life.

To maintain a resilient mindset, consider these approaches:

- Integrate affirmations and positive self-talk into your daily routine. Whether it's in the morning before you start your day, during breaks from studying, or right before bed, consistency is key.

- Surround yourself with positivity. Engage with people who uplift you and avoid those who drain your energy or reinforce negative thinking.

- Reflect on your progress periodically. Recognize improvements in your thought patterns and celebrate small victories along the way.

- Balance self-compassion with personal responsibility. Understand that while it's important to acknowledge hardships and give yourself grace, you must also hold yourself accountable for putting in the effort needed to succeed.

The key takeaway here is that positive self-talk and affirmations are not just fluffy concepts; they are tangible tools grounded in cognitive-behavioral principles. These practices help boost self-esteem, foster a positive attitude, and manage anxiety through constructive inner dialogue.

By systematically implementing these strategies, you move beyond merely coping with exam stress —you actively reshape your mental landscape to one of strength and assurance. It's about setting up a strong psychological foundation that supports not only your academic endeavors but also your overall well-being.

Incorporating these methods into your exam preparation routine can make a world of difference. They offer practical, evidence-based techniques to help you build confidence and approach your exams with a positive mindset. Remember, it's not just about passing an exam; it's about cultivating a resilient, empowered state of mind that benefits all areas of your life.

Practicing Visualization Techniques for Success

Imagine yourself walking into the exam room with a sense of calm, confidence, and poise. The first teaching focuses on visualizing this serene approach to exams, which can significantly reduce anxiety and boost performance. Picture yourself handling each challenge that comes your way with ease and composure. Here's how you can start:

- Find a quiet place where you won't be disturbed.
- Close your eyes and take a few deep breaths, allowing your body to relax.
- Visualize the moment you enter the exam room. Notice the details around you—the arrangement of desks, the sound of footsteps, and the rustling of papers.
- See yourself feeling composed and confident, as you walk to your seat and prepare for the exam.
- Imagine reading through the questions calmly, understanding them clearly, and knowing exactly what to do next.
- Envision yourself effectively managing time and tackling each question with assurance.

By practicing this visualization, you prime your mind to experience exams in a positive, calm manner. It can reshape how you perceive these situations, turning anxiety-inducing moments into opportunities for demonstrating competence and resilience.

Transitioning to the next teaching, it involves creating mental images of achieving your desired outcomes. This is about painting a picture of success in your mind. Visualize receiving the grades you aspire to achieve or feeling a deep sense of pride after completing the exam. Here are some steps to guide you:

- Again, find a quiet environment and close your eyes.
- Use vivid imagery to see yourself holding the exam paper with excellent grades.
- Imagine the sense of accomplishment you feel as you realize your hard work has paid off.
- Picture sharing the good news with family and friends, sensing their pride and support.
- Feel the joy and satisfaction that comes from seeing your efforts bear fruit.

This kind of visualization helps anchor your goals in your subconscious mind, making them more tangible and achievable. By repeatedly imagining successful outcomes, you reinforce your belief in your ability to succeed, which can translate into improved performance during the actual exam.

Next, we delve into the importance of sensory details in your visualization practice. Engaging all your senses makes the experience more vivid and impactful. When you visualize, don't just see the images; try to hear the sounds, smell the scents, and feel the emotions. Here's how you can amplify your visualization:

- As you visualize walking into the exam room, listen to the ambient noises—the hum of air conditioning, the shuffle of feet.
- Feel the texture of the desk under your fingers and the smoothness of the pen you're using.
- Smell the clean, yet slightly musty scent of the room, or perhaps the faint aroma of coffee on your breath.
- Hear the gentle rustle of paper as you turn the pages of the exam booklet.
- Experience the emotion of calm confidence washing over you, easing any tension in your muscles.

Integrating sensory details not only enhances the realism of your visualization but also creates stronger neural connections in your brain. This immersion helps your mind accept the scenario as familiar and achievable, further reducing anxiety and bolstering self-assurance.

Finally, let's explore incorporating relaxation techniques into your visualization practice. Combining imagery with deep breathing or progressive muscle relaxation can enhance its effectiveness. This combination can help relax both your body and mind, creating a powerful tool against anxiety. Here's a method to integrate relaxation techniques:

- Begin by sitting comfortably in a quiet place. Close your eyes and take slow, deep breaths.
- Start with deep breathing: Inhale deeply through your nose, hold for a few seconds, then exhale slowly through your mouth. Repeat this a few times.
- As you breathe, begin to visualize the exam scenario. Recall the detailed imagery we've discussed earlier.
- With each inhale, imagine drawing in calmness and confidence.
- With each exhale, envision releasing anxiety and tension.
- Progress to muscle relaxation: Starting from your toes, tense each muscle group for a few seconds, then release. Move upwards through your legs, abdomen, chest, arms, shoulders, and finally your neck and face.
- Simultaneously visualize the exam scene, merging the calming effect of physical relaxation with the soothing power of positive imagery.

Practicing these combined techniques regularly conditions your mind and body to remain calm and focused under pressure. It's like rehearsing for the big day, so when it arrives, you're well-prepared and equipped to handle it with grace.

The key takeaway from this section is that visualization exercises can be incredibly effective in improving performance, boosting self-assurance, and reducing test-related anxiety. By mentally preparing yourself for success, you create a mindset that views challenges as manageable and surmountable.

Remember, the power of visualization lies in consistency. The more you practice, the more ingrained these positive scenarios become in your psyche. Visualization isn't a one-time fix; it's a habit to cultivate. Approach it with patience and persistence, and you'll likely notice a significant shift in your exam experiences.

Combining visualization with other cognitive-behavioral strategies can further enhance its impact. Each technique you adopt adds another layer of resilience, helping you build a robust toolkit for managing stress and excelling under pressure. By investing time in these practices, you empower yourself to transform anxiety into a catalyst for success.

Utilizing Relaxation Response Methods

One of the most effective ways to manage stress and anxiety, particularly in high-pressure situations like exams, is through diaphragmatic breathing exercises. This technique helps elicit the body's relaxation response, counteracting the fight-or-flight reaction often triggered by exam pressure. Here's how you can incorporate this practice:

- Find a quiet space where you won't be disturbed.
- Sit or lie down in a comfortable position.
- Place one hand on your chest and the other on your abdomen.
- Inhale deeply through your nose, allowing your diaphragm (not your chest) to expand with air. You should feel your abdomen rise more than your chest.
- Exhale slowly through your mouth.

Practicing this exercise for just a few minutes can significantly reduce anxiety levels and leave you feeling more centered and calm. Taking regular breaks during study sessions to focus on your breathing can help maintain steady progress and mental clarity.

Another valuable method to release tension is engaging in progressive muscle relaxation (PMR). This technique involves systematically tensing and then relaxing different muscle groups in your body. It not only promotes physical relaxation but also alleviates symptoms of anxiety and nervousness. To practice PMR:

- Find a quiet place where you can sit or lie down comfortably.
- Start with your toes: press them down hard into the floor or curl them tightly, hold for a few seconds, then release.
- Move up to your calves, thighs, abdomen, arms, shoulders, and finally your face, progressively tensing each area for five to ten seconds before releasing.

By focusing on the process of tensing and relaxing each muscle group, you can shift your mind away from anxious thoughts and sensations, achieving a state of deep physical and mental relaxation. Incorporating PMR into your daily routine can prepare you to handle exam-related stress more effectively.

In addition to breathing and muscle relaxation techniques, mindfulness-based stress reduction (MBSR) practices, such as body scans and focused breathing, are excellent for enhancing awareness, presence, and emotional regulation. These practices can be especially beneficial during exams, helping you stay grounded and composed. Here's how to incorporate MBSR into your routine:

- Body Scan: Lie down in a comfortable position. Close your eyes and take a few deep breaths. Gradually bring your attention to different parts of your body, starting from your toes and moving upwards. Notice any sensations, tension, or discomfort. Simply observe these feelings without judgment and then move on to the next part of your body.
- Focused Breathing: Sit comfortably with your back straight. Close your eyes and take a few deep breaths. Focus your attention entirely on your breath—the sensation of air entering and leaving your nostrils, the rise and fall of your chest, and the rhythm of your breathing. If your mind wanders, gently bring it back to your breath.

Regular practice of mindfulness techniques cultivates presence and emotional balance, making it easier to manage stress and maintain focus during exams.

Establishing a pre-exam relaxation routine can significantly enhance your ability to manage anxiety effectively. This routine might include deep breathing, visualization, or brief mindfulness exercises. Visualize yourself sitting calmly and confidently during the exam, knowing that you are prepared and capable. Pair this mental imagery with deep, rhythmic breathing to create a sense of calm and readiness.

To put together an effective pre-exam relaxation routine:

- Begin with a few minutes of diaphragmatic breathing to center yourself.
- Follow this with a brief session of progressive muscle relaxation to release any residual tension.
- Conclude with a mindful visualization exercise where you picture yourself succeeding in the exam environment.

This comprehensive approach ensures that you enter the exam feeling balanced, focused, and equipped to perform to the best of your ability.

Integrating these relaxation response methods—diaphragmatic breathing, progressive muscle relaxation, mindfulness-based stress reduction practices, and a pre-exam routine—into your exam preparation not only helps reduce stress levels but also improves concentration and enhances performance. By adopting these practices, you foster a calm and centered state of mind, which is crucial for navigating the pressures of academic assessments.

In our evidence-driven world, it's essential to recognize the profound impact of these techniques, supported by empirical research, on improving human welfare. Balancing economic growth and personal well-being, especially for adult students and professionals seeking further education, requires acknowledging the importance of mental health strategies like these. They serve as both a tool for personal responsibility and a part of the safety net needed when facing life's inevitable challenges.

As we move towards a more holistic approach to education and professional development, incorporating such practical strategies becomes indispensable. By doing so, we don't just aim for academic success; we strive for overall well-being, creating a healthier, more resilient society. Through these methods, we empower individuals to take control of their mental health, fostering environments where learning and personal growth can flourish harmoniously.

Integrating Cognitive-Behavioral Strategies for Test Success

In this chapter, we have explored various cognitive-behavioral strategies designed to help you reframe negative thoughts and reduce anxiety levels, particularly in the context of exam preparation. By identifying and challenging irrational beliefs, replacing them with rational thoughts, practicing self-compassion, and utilizing cognitive restructuring, you can build a more positive and confident mindset.

We began by understanding how irrational beliefs, such as fearing failure or feeling inadequate, can cause significant stress and negatively impact performance. By writing down these negative thoughts, gathering evidence to challenge them, and comparing them with facts, you can discover that these beliefs often lack validity. Replacing them with balanced perspectives helps cultivate a more constructive outlook.

Further, methods like self-compassion prompt you to treat yourself kindly during moments of doubt, fostering acceptance rather than criticism. Cognitive restructuring encourages you to shape your thoughts in a way that enhances both your emotional state and your approach to stressful situations.

The chapter also highlighted the importance of positive self-talk and affirmations. These practical tools enable you to manage anxiety by creating a mental script that emphasizes readiness and competence. Practicing visualization techniques prepares your mind for success by vividly imagining positive scenarios and outcomes, which can diminish anxiety and boost exam performance.

Relaxation response methods, such as diaphragmatic breathing, progressive muscle relaxation, and mindfulness-based practices, provide effective ways to relieve stress and maintain focus. Establishing a pre-exam relaxation routine incorporating these techniques ensures you enter the exam room calm, centered, and prepared.

However, it is important to remember that adopting these strategies requires consistency and patience. Implementing these cognitive-behavioral techniques doesn't yield instant results but offers long-term benefits in managing anxiety and building self-confidence. For some, seeking additional support from a therapist or counselor trained in cognitive-behavioral therapy may be beneficial.

Ultimately, the ability to manage your thoughts and emotions positively impacts not only your exam performance but also other areas of life. Developing these skills contributes to overall mental well-being and resilience, equipping you to handle various high-pressure situations with greater ease.

As you continue practicing these methods, keep in mind that exams are just one moment in time—they do not define your worth or intelligence. Your genuine effort, resilience, and ability to adapt are far more indicative of your potential and capability. The journey towards mastering these cognitive-behavioral strategies is ongoing, and every step you take brings you closer to a more empowered and confident version of yourself.

Chapter 3

Mastering Mindfulness Practices

In the fast-paced realm of academic success, the pressure to perform well in exams can often feel overwhelming. Students and professionals alike grapple with stress, struggling to maintain focus amidst a whirlwind of thoughts and distractions. Yet, within this chaos lies an age-old practice offering solace and stability: mindfulness. Mindfulness, rooted in ancient traditions yet backed by modern science, provides techniques to center the mind, enhance concentration, and foster a sense of calm. As you delve into these practices, you'll discover how subtle shifts in awareness can lead to profound changes in your exam preparation and performance.

Exam anxiety manifests in myriad ways—sweaty palms, racing hearts, and minds that spiral into worst-case scenarios. These responses, though natural, can severely hinder performance. Imagine sitting down for a critical test, only to find your mind blank or preoccupied with worries about failure. The inability to focus on the task at hand is not just frustrating but can be debilitating. This chapter addresses such concerns by offering practical solutions to manage these stressful moments. By observing your thoughts as they arise without judgment, you create space for better focus and clarity, significantly reducing the likelihood of panic and mental blocks during exams.

This chapter will introduce several mindfulness exercises designed specifically to enhance focus, reduce stress, and cultivate a sense of calm. Through guided practices like mindful breathing, body scans, and the non-judgmental observation of thoughts and emotions, you'll learn how to navigate the pressures of exam situations more effectively. Each technique will be explained clearly, providing step-by-step instructions to help you integrate mindfulness into your daily routine. By doing so, you're not only preparing for exams but also equipping yourself with lifelong skills to handle stress and maintain mental clarity in any challenging situation.

Introduction to Mindfulness Meditation

Mindfulness meditation involves focusing on the present moment without judgment. This practice can help individuals increase their awareness of thoughts, emotions, and bodily sensations, promoting a sense of calmness and clarity.

By introducing readers to mindfulness meditation, they can learn to observe their thoughts without getting entangled in them, leading to improved concentration and reduced anxiety during exams. Often, during high-stress moments like exams, our minds tend to spiral into negative thinking or overwhelming worry. Mindfulness meditation offers a way out of that loop. By practicing mindfulness, you can gain the ability to separate yourself from your thoughts, creating space for better focus and calmness.

Here's how you can observe your thoughts without getting entangled in them:

- Begin by finding a quiet and comfortable place to sit. Close your eyes and take a few deep breaths.

- Focus on your breath as it comes in and goes out. Feel the sensation of the air entering your nostrils, filling your lungs, and leaving your body.

- As you do this, thoughts will inevitably arise. When they do, simply acknowledge them without judgment and let them go. Imagine your thoughts as clouds passing through the sky. You see them, but you don't need to interact with them.

- Return your focus to your breathing each time you notice your mind wandering. It might happen repeatedly, and that's completely okay. The practice is about gently bringing your attention back.

Practicing this regularly will enhance your ability to stay present and focused, particularly during stressful situations like exams. It becomes easier to manage anxieties and maintain clarity, which are crucial for optimal performance.

Furthermore, practicing mindfulness meditation regularly can enhance self-regulation skills and promote emotional resilience in challenging situations. When we talk about self-regulation, it's the ability to manage our emotions, thoughts, and behaviors effectively in different circumstances. Regular mindfulness practice trains your brain to respond rather than react impulsively. You'll find that over time, you become more adept at handling stress, making thoughtful decisions under pressure, and staying composed even in the most trying times.

Emotional resilience, on the other hand, is about bouncing back from adversity. It's not just about enduring tough times but thriving despite them. Mindfulness helps build this resilience by fostering a non-reactive awareness and acceptance of your current experience. By consistently practicing mindfulness, you cultivate an inner strength that makes you less susceptible to being knocked off course by stress or anxiety.

Readers can develop a daily mindfulness meditation routine to build a foundation for inner peace and mental clarity. Establishing a regular practice routine is essential for reaping the full benefits of mindfulness. Here's a simple guideline to get you started on creating a daily mindfulness meditation habit:

- Choose a consistent time each day that works best for you. Early mornings or just before bed are common choices, but what's most important is picking a time you can stick to.

- Start with a short duration, especially if you are new to meditation. Even 5 to 10 minutes can make a significant difference. Gradually increase the duration as you become more comfortable.

- Create a dedicated space for your practice. It doesn't have to be elaborate; a simple corner of a room where you won't be disturbed can work wonders.

- Use a timer to avoid checking the clock. There are many apps available designed specifically for meditation timers, offering gentle sounds to start and end your sessions.

- Integrate mindfulness into your daily activities. Whether it's mindful eating, walking, or even brushing your teeth, try to bring a state of mindful awareness to these activities.

Incorporating such practices into your daily life allows mindfulness to become more than just a scheduled activity. It starts to permeate your entire day, helping you maintain a state of calm and focus continuously. Especially for adult students or professionals gearing up for exams, having this steady anchor can drastically reduce the overwhelm and provide a clearer, more balanced perspective.

Developing a daily mindfulness meditation routine ensures you build a strong foundation of inner peace and mental clarity, which are invaluable assets, especially in high-pressure environments like exam settings. With time, you'll notice changes not only in how you handle test anxiety but also in various other aspects of your life. Mindfulness isn't just a tool for specific moments; it's a lifelong skill that enhances overall well-being.

So, as you embark on your journey of mindfulness, remember it's about progress, not perfection. Each time you sit down to meditate, you are nurturing your mind, preparing it for the challenges ahead, and setting yourself up for success. Start small, stay consistent, and be kind to yourself throughout the process. The rewards, though subtle at first, will undoubtedly manifest in profound ways, ensuring you face exams—and life—with greater calm, focus, and resilience.

Embarking on this journey can bring about profound change. Not only will mindfulness offer immediate relief from exam-related stress, but it will also cultivate a stable and resilient mind capable of navigating life's numerous challenges. Armed with these strategies, you're not just preparing for exams; you're equipping yourself with tools for a healthier, more centered approach to all future endeavors.

Body Scan and Breathing Techniques for Relaxation

Let's delve into how you can use mindfulness exercises to enhance focus, reduce stress, and cultivate a sense of calm during exams.

First up is body scan meditation. This technique involves systematically focusing on different parts of the body to release tension and promote relaxation. Start by finding a quiet, comfortable place where you won't be disturbed. Sit or lie down with your eyes closed. Begin by taking a few deep breaths to help center yourself. Then, shift your attention to your toes. Notice any sensations, tension, or discomfort and allow them to soften. Slowly move your focus up through your feet, legs, torso, arms, and head, pausing at each body part to observe and release tension. The aim here is not to change anything but to become aware of how your body feels and to invite relaxation.

- Locate a quiet space where you won't be interrupted.
- Choose a comfortable position, either sitting or lying down.
- Close your eyes and take a few deep breaths to ease into the practice.
- Direct your focus to your toes, observing any sensations and releasing tension.
- Gradually move attention upward through each body part, one at a time.
- Allow yourself to fully experience and then let go of any tension in each area.

Teaching readers breathing techniques such as diaphragmatic breathing can regulate the body's stress response and induce a state of relaxation. Diaphragmatic breathing, also known as belly breathing, involves deep, mindful breaths that engage the diaphragm rather than shallow ones involving only the chest. To practice this, sit comfortably with your back straight or lie down if you prefer. Place one hand on your chest and the other on your abdomen. Breathe in deeply through your nose, allowing your abdomen to rise while keeping your chest relatively still. Exhale slowly through your mouth. Repeat this process several times, focusing on the sensation of your breath entering and leaving your body. This can counteract the physiological effects of anxiety and improve focus.

- Sit upright or lie down comfortably, ensuring your back is straight.
- Rest one hand on your chest and the other on your abdomen.
- Inhale deeply through your nose, allowing your abdomen to rise rather than your chest.
- Exhale slowly and fully through your mouth.
- Focus on the rhythm of your breath and repeat several times.

By incorporating body scan and breathing exercises into your exam preparation routine, you can establish a vital connection between mind and body, fostering a sense of peace and centeredness. As you practice these techniques regularly, you'll likely notice an improvement in your overall mental well-being. These exercises provide a way to take control of your thoughts and emotions, grounding yourself in the present moment and reducing the impact of stressful future events.

Practicing these techniques before exams can create a calm internal environment conducive to optimal cognitive functioning and performance. Consider setting aside a specific time each day to engage in these mindfulness practices, particularly in the lead-up to your exams. By making them a regular part of your routine, you're training your mind and body to respond more calmly under pressure. This doesn't just improve your immediate sense of well-being; it also enhances your ability to think clearly and perform more effectively when it matters most.

The beauty of these mindfulness techniques lies in their simplicity and effectiveness. They don't require any special equipment or a significant amount of time—just a commitment to prioritizing your mental health. When combined with other study strategies, these practices can significantly impact your readiness and resilience during exam periods.

In summary, integrating mindfulness exercises like body scan meditation and diaphragmatic breathing into your daily routine can bolster your capacity to handle exam-related stress. These methods are grounded in empirical evidence and have been shown to reduce anxiety, enhance focus, and promote a state of calm. By dedicating a few minutes each day to practice these techniques, you can cultivate a balanced approach to exam preparation that supports both your academic goals and your well-being.

Mindful Awareness of Thoughts and Emotions

Mindful awareness involves observing thoughts and emotions with non-judgmental acceptance. When we sit for exams, a whirlwind of worries and self-doubt can cloud our focus. By cultivating the skill of mindful observation, students can recognize these apprehensions without getting swept up in them. This practice allows for a clearer mind, which is essential in high-stakes situations like exams.

Teaching readers to acknowledge their thoughts and emotions without reacting impulsively can prevent the escalation of anxiety during exams. Here is what you can do to achieve this:

- Start by acknowledging your feelings as they arise. If you feel anxious, simply note it mentally: "I'm feeling anxious," without judgment.

- Take a deep breath and bring your attention to the present moment. Focus on your breathing for a few cycles, which helps anchor your mind.

- Allow yourself to feel your anxiety. Rather than pushing it away or reacting impulsively (e.g., panicking, reviewing notes frantically), observe it from an objective standpoint. Imagine you're a scientist studying your own reactions.

- Practice this regularly, not just during exams but also in everyday life. Frequent practice makes it easier to employ these skills when under pressure.

By developing this skill, readers can manage test-related anxieties more effectively. This approach fosters a balanced perspective and emotional stability. The anxiety doesn't vanish, but it becomes something manageable rather than overwhelming.

Cultivating the ability to stay present and observe internal experiences empowers individuals to respond to exam pressures mindfully. Imagine being in an exam room, the clock ticking ominously, and you encounter a difficult question. Instead of spiraling into a stress reaction, you can pause and bring yourself back to the present moment. Observe your initial anxious response without trying to suppress it. Notice how this acknowledgment gives you space to make a thoughtful decision instead of succumbing to panic.

The act of staying present equips you with the mental resilience needed to navigate exam challenges skillfully. It's important to understand that mindfulness isn't about eliminating stress; it's about changing our relationship with stress. When we confront academic hurdles with clear minds and calm dispositions, we are better positioned to find effective solutions.

Encouraging readers to practice mindful awareness during test-taking moments enables them to stay focused, maintain composure, and approach challenges with a clear mind. To practice this effectively, consider these guidelines:

- Before starting the exam, close your eyes for a moment and take several deep breaths. Ground yourself by feeling the contact between your body and the chair.

- When you start the exam, read each question mindfully. Pay full attention to the words and allow yourself to process the information slowly.

- If you feel your mind wandering or racing, gently bring your focus back to your breath or the task at hand. It's natural for the mind to wander; the key is to keep returning to the present moment.

- During breaks or pauses, practice brief moments of mindful breathing or stretching. This helps reset your focus and reduces accumulated tension.

The power of mindfulness lies in its simplicity. These practices can be seamlessly integrated into your exam routine without requiring extensive time or effort. They serve as micro-moments of calm that collectively build a resilient mindset.

Observing thoughts and emotions with non-judgmental acceptance, in itself, cultivates a nurturing environment for personal growth. When students accept their thoughts and feelings without rushing to label them as 'good' or 'bad,' they open themselves up to genuine understanding. This deeper insight into one's emotional landscape can then be leveraged to foster a healthier attitude towards exams and other stress-inducing scenarios.

Imagine you're facing an intense bout of nerves before an important test. By merely noting the physical sensations—like a rapid heartbeat or sweaty palms—and recognizing the accompanying thoughts, you defuse their power. You realize these are transient states rather than fixed realities. This realization can be profoundly liberating, helping you to approach the exam with a more composed and centered mindset.

Furthermore, mindful awareness is not just beneficial for the moments leading up to and during exams. Its benefits extend well beyond, offering a lifetime skill that can be applied in various stressful situations—professional settings, personal relationships, or any circumstances that demand emotional resilience.

When encountering challenging questions during an exam, maintaining mindful awareness can be a game-changer. Instead of reacting with immediate stress and frustration, you can take a step back. Recognize your emotional and cognitive responses, and address them with curiosity rather than judgment. For instance, if you feel stuck on a particularly tough question, take a moment to breathe deeply, refocus, and approach it from a fresh angle. This shift in perspective often uncovers new pathways to the solution.

Through consistent practice, students can develop a sense of inner calm that remains accessible even during high-pressure moments. This sense of calm empowers them to navigate exams with poise and confidence, reducing the likelihood of anxiety-driven mistakes.

Moreover, mindfulness encourages a broader view of success. It emphasizes effort and process over outcome, reminding us that exams are just one aspect of our educational journey. By embracing this mindset, students alleviate the all-or-nothing thinking that often exacerbates stress.

Incorporating mindfulness into exam preparation can yield significant benefits. Begin with small steps, such as dedicating a few minutes each day to mindful breathing or meditation. Gradually extend these practices and incorporate them into study sessions or mock exams. Over time, the habits will become second nature, providing a robust foundation for managing exam-related stress.

Remember, the essence of mindfulness lies in practice, not perfection. Each attempt to bring mindfulness into your exam routine enhances your ability to manage stress and perform optimally. The more you engage in these practices, the stronger your mental and emotional fortitude will become.

In conclusion, utilizing mindfulness exercises is a powerful strategy for enhancing focus, reducing stress, and cultivating a sense of calm during exams. By observing thoughts and emotions with non-judgmental acceptance, acknowledging feelings without impulsive reactions, staying present, and practicing mindfulness during test-taking moments, students can significantly improve their performance and well-being. These techniques, rooted in empirical evidence, offer practical tools for navigating the complexities of academic exams with confidence and clarity.

Utilizing Mindfulness in Test-Taking Situations

Applying mindfulness techniques during exams helps individuals stay grounded and attentive, mitigating distractions and enhancing concentration on the task at hand. Exam stress is something many of us are familiar with – the sweaty palms, racing thoughts, and the sheer dread of forgetting everything we've studied. But mindfulness can be an effective tool to counter these sensations, promoting a composed and focused mindset.

To begin with, consider employing mindful breathing. This straightforward technique doesn't require any special equipment or prior experience. When you find your mind wandering or panic setting in, focus on your breath. Pay close attention to the sensation of air entering your nostrils, filling your lungs, and then leaving your body. This deliberate attention to breath can act as an anchor, pulling your focus away from anxiety-inducing thoughts and back to the present moment.

Here's what you can do to apply mindful breathing effectively during exams:

- Close your eyes for a moment if it feels comfortable and inhale deeply through the nose.
- Feel the expansion of your abdomen and chest and hold your breath for a brief second.
- Exhale slowly and thoroughly through your mouth, ensuring all the air is expelled.
- Repeat this process a few times until you notice a change in your tension levels and focus.

Moreover, body awareness exercises can also be incredibly beneficial. Often, stress manifests physically – tight shoulders, clenched jaws, or a stiff neck. Conducting a quick body scan during an exam can help you identify and release these points of tension. Start by focusing on your feet; feel the contact they make with the ground. Gradually move up to your legs, torso, arms, and finally, your head. This practice helps shift the focus from your racing mind to your physical state, aiding in relaxation and clarity.

When faced with overwhelming stress or performance anxiety, it's essential to have a toolkit of coping strategies at your disposal. Mindfulness practices such as those mentioned above can serve as these tools. The essence of mindfulness lies in its ability to bring us back to the present, reminding us that we are not our thoughts or fears, but observers of them. By practicing techniques like mindful breathing and body awareness, you're better equipped to handle whatever comes your way during exams.

Integrating mindfulness into test-taking scenarios manages nerves, regulates emotions, and maintains a positive mindset, leading to improved performance outcomes. Imagine walking into the exam room devoid of the usual apprehension. Instead, you feel calm, collected, and ready to face the challenge head-on. By bringing mindfulness into the equation, you essentially train your brain to operate more efficiently under pressure.

Here's how you can start integrating mindfulness into your test-taking routine:

- Before starting the exam, take a moment to sit quietly, focusing on your breath or performing a quick body scan.
- During the exam, if you feel your anxiety rising, pause briefly, close your eyes, and take three slow, deep breaths.
- Trust in your preparation and recognize that worrying about the outcome will only hinder your performance. Shift your focus back to the question at hand.

Consistent practice of these techniques doesn't just offer temporary relief. It fosters a habit of presence and resilience, enabling individuals to navigate academic challenges with confidence and clarity. Think of mindfulness as a muscle that strengthens over time. The more you engage in mindfulness practices, the more natural and automatic they become, especially in stressful situations like exams.

Regularly incorporating these practices outside of exam situations can reinforce their effectiveness. Consider setting aside a few minutes each day to practice mindfulness. Over time, you'll likely notice not just a reduction in exam-related stress, but an overall improvement in your ability to manage daily stresses and maintain focus.

In conclusion, the busy world we live in often pushes us to perform without necessarily equipping us with the tools to manage the accompanying stress. However, mindfulness offers a pragmatic and evidence-based approach to dealing with exam anxiety, allowing you to remain grounded, attentive, and composed. By investing time in cultivating these practices, you're not only enhancing your exam performance but also contributing to long-term mental well-being. Remember, every breath and every moment of awareness brings you closer to mastering your inner environment, no matter what external pressures come your way.

Integrating Mindfulness for Exam Success

In this chapter, we explored how mindfulness exercises can enhance focus, reduce stress, and cultivate a sense of calm during exams. Starting from the foundational practice of mindfulness meditation, we delved into techniques like body scan, diaphragmatic breathing, and mindful awareness of thoughts and emotions. Each of these practices provides tools to manage test anxiety, promote emotional resilience, and maintain mental clarity.

Referring back to the introduction, we emphasized how mindfulness can help you observe your thoughts without getting caught up in them, leading to better concentration and less anxiety. Our current position underscores that regular mindfulness practice indeed fortifies your ability to stay present and composed, particularly during high-stakes situations like exams.

While embracing mindfulness can be transformative, it's essential to acknowledge some challenges. For instance, maintaining a consistent practice can be difficult amidst busy schedules, and initial attempts may feel discouraging if the immediate benefits aren't noticeable. However, perseverance in integrating these techniques can provide profound, long-lasting advantages beyond exams, touching various aspects of life including professional settings and personal relationships.

On a broader scale, adopting mindfulness can contribute to a more balanced and focused approach to stress management. As society increasingly demands high performance under pressure, fostering such skills can lead to healthier individuals who are more adept at navigating both academic and professional challenges.

As you continue on your mindfulness journey, consider each practice session as an investment in your mental and emotional well-being. The goal is not perfection but progress. Take solace in knowing that every moment dedicated to mindfulness is a step toward greater calm, resilience, and focus, equipping you with valuable tools for future endeavors.

The next time you face an exam, or any stressful situation, remember the power of being present. Embrace the moment with mindful awareness and watch how it transforms your approach and outcomes.

Chapter 4

Breathing Exercisesfor Test Confidence

The sound of your heart pounding in your chest, the shallow breaths that seem to quicken with every second, and the persistent flutter of nerves in your stomach—these are familiar sensations to anyone who has faced the pressure of an impending exam. Imagine having a simple tool at your disposal that could transform that tension into a sense of calm and control, one breath at a time. This chapter offers just that—a collection of breathing exercises designed to help you manage test anxiety and boost your confidence, allowing you to navigate exams with greater ease.

Exam stress is a common hurdle for adult students and professionals alike, often manifesting in both mental and physical symptoms. Think about the moments before an exam when your mind races through worst-case scenarios, or during the test itself when a challenging question triggers a wave of panic. These reactions can cloud your judgment, impair your focus, and ultimately affect your performance. For instance, Joe, a mid-career professional aspiring for certification, found himself paralyzed by these anxiety symptoms despite his extensive preparation. His experience isn't unique; many face similar struggles that undermine their true potential.

In this chapter, we will delve into various breathing techniques that can be seamlessly incorporated into your routine to mitigate these anxiety symptoms. From deep breathing to diaphragmatic methods and alternate nostril exercises, each technique is explained in detail, offering practical steps and the science behind how they work. You will discover strategies to implement these exercises both as part of your daily regimen and in high-pressure situations like exams. The goal is to equip you with tools to reclaim your peace of mind, enhance focus, and approach tests with newfound confidence.

Deep Breathing Techniques

It's no secret that exams can be a significant source of stress and anxiety for many adult students. Whether you're returning to school after years in the workforce or pursuing further certifications to advance your career, the pressure to perform well can feel overwhelming. One practical strategy to manage this stress effectively is through deep breathing exercises. These techniques not only help calm the mind and body but also instill a sense of control and confidence, crucial during high-stakes situations like exams.

Deep breathing involves a simple yet powerful process that activates the body's relaxation response. Here's how you can do it:

- **Inhale slowly through your nose** , allowing your abdomen to expand as you fill your lungs with air.

- **Hold your breath for a few seconds** , generally counting up to four or five.

- **Exhale gently through your mouth** , ensuring the exhale is slower than the inhale.

This method works by stimulating the parasympathetic nervous system, which counteracts the body's fight-or-flight response triggered by anxiety. By practicing this sequence, you can shift your physiological state from one of heightened alertness to one of calming repose.

In moments of acute stress, such as right before an exam or during a particularly challenging question, deep breathing can be a lifesaver. When anxiety strikes, it often manifests physically—your heart races, your muscles tense, and your breath becomes shallow and rapid. Engaging in deep breathing helps to recalibrate your nervous system, reducing these physical symptoms. This action creates a feedback loop where calming the body contributes to calming the mind, allowing you to regain focus and composure.

Here is what you can do in order to achieve the goal:

- **Pause** whatever you're doing at the first sign of mounting stress.
- **Focus on your breathing** by directing your attention inward. Start with a slow inhale through your nose.
- **Count silently as you hold your breath** —this small mental activity shifts focus away from anxiety-inducing thoughts.
- **Exhale slowly and completely** , emptying your lungs of all the air.
- Repeat the cycle a few times until you notice your heartbeat slowing and muscles relaxing.

What's more, these deep breathing techniques can be done discreetly in the exam room itself. Suppose you're mid-exam, feeling the pressure building up, find yourself a quiet moment to engage in a few cycles of deep breathing. The beauty of this practice lies in its subtlety; others around you won't even realize you're employing a coping mechanism. By managing your stress levels on the spot, you can maintain your focus and keep anxiety-induced errors at bay.

Furthermore, incorporating deep breathing into your daily routine can cultivate longer-term resilience against test anxiety. Regular practice trains your body to respond more calmly under pressure, creating a foundation of emotional stability. Consider integrating deep breathing exercises into your morning or evening routines.

Guidelines to incorporate deep breathing into your daily life:

- **Start your day** with a brief session of deep breathing. Just five minutes in the morning can set a positive tone for the rest of the day.
- **Take short breaks** throughout your day to practice deep breathing. These mini-sessions can serve as a quick reset during stressful periods.
- **End your day** with another round of deep breathing. This helps transition your mind and body into a relaxed state conducive to restful sleep.
- **Combine deep breathing with other relaxation techniques** like meditation or progressive muscle relaxation for enhanced benefits.

By making this a habit, you're essentially training your nervous system to remain balanced, even in stressful scenarios.

The consistent practice of these exercises fosters a reliable coping mechanism for anxiety, enhancing your overall sense of control during exams. It's like having an internal reset button that you can press anytime things start to feel overwhelming. Moreover, this learned skill extends beyond exams and can be utilized in various high-pressure situations, be it delivering a presentation at work or navigating personal challenges.

To sum up, deep breathing exercises offer a practical, evidence-based way to manage test anxiety. By learning to control your breathing, you can activate your body's natural relaxation response, calm your nervous system, and reduce the physical symptoms of anxiety. The ability to perform this technique discreetly in the exam room ensures you can maintain focus and control even when faced with difficult questions. And by implementing deep breathing into your daily routine, you build a resilience that not only aids in exam performance but also contributes to overall well-being.

Give it a try. The next time you feel the weight of exam stress pressing down, pause, breathe deeply, and reclaim your peace of mind. You may find that this simple technique not only improves your performance but also leaves you feeling more empowered and confident in the face of challenges.

Diaphragmatic Breathing Techniques

Diaphragmatic breathing involves breathing deeply into the abdomen, expanding the diaphragm to fully oxygenate the body and release tension. This technique is widely recognized in both scientific literature and clinical practice as an effective method for reducing anxiety and promoting relaxation. Here's how you can implement this practice to help manage stress and maintain composure during exams:

- **Find a quiet place** where you won't be disturbed for a few minutes.
- **Sit or lie down comfortably** , ensuring your back is straight if sitting.
- **Place one hand on your chest and the other on your abdomen** , just below your rib cage.
- **Inhale slowly through your nose** , allowing your abdomen (not your chest) to rise as you fill your lungs with air.
- **Exhale gently through your mouth** , letting the air flow out naturally while feeling your abdomen fall.

Practicing diaphragmatic breathing exercises regularly trains the body to respond calmly to stressors and maintain focus under pressure. It's important to integrate this practice into your daily routine so it becomes second nature. By doing so, you can condition your body to activate this relaxation response automatically in stressful situations, such as taking exams or dealing with unexpected challenges.

Regular practice doesn't have to be time-consuming. You can incorporate short sessions of diaphragmatic breathing into your day. Start with a few minutes each morning and evening, gradually increasing the duration as you become more comfortable. Over time, your body will learn to adopt this calmer state more quickly and efficiently.

Adopting diaphragmatic breathing as a tool to center oneself before exams can promote a sense of calm and confidence in one's abilities. When you face the exam room's intimidating environment, a brief session of focused breathing can help anchor your mind and body. Taking a few deep, controlled breaths can signal your nervous system to de-escalate any rising tension, creating a mental space where you feel more in control and less prone to anxiety.

Utilizing diaphragmatic breathing as a quick and effective way to manage test anxiety symptoms and maintain a clear mindset during exams is practical and accessible. In the midst of an exam, you might encounter moments where nerves spike and clarity fades. A swift return to diaphragmatic breathing can act as a reset button, helping you regain focus and proceed with greater ease.

In essence, diaphragmatic breathing is a powerful technique for individuals to relax their body and mind, fostering a conducive environment for exam success and confidence. This simple yet effective method can empower you to take control of your physiological responses to stress, ensuring that anxiety does not overshadow your preparation and performance. By integrating this practice into your routine and utilizing it during crucial moments, you set the groundwork for a calmer, more confident approach to exams.

Understanding the mechanics and benefits of diaphragmatic breathing provides a foundation, but the true effectiveness lies in consistent practice. The more you engage in these exercises, the more ingrained they become, offering reliable support in times of need. It's about building a habit that aligns with your physiological need for balance and calm, especially when facing high-pressure scenarios like exams.

Moreover, research supports the efficacy of diaphragmatic breathing in reducing symptoms of anxiety and improving overall well-being. Studies have shown that those who practice this form of breathing regularly exhibit lower levels of cortisol, the stress hormone, and increased activity in parts of the brain associated with emotional regulation and cognitive function.

Consider, for instance, a study conducted by Harvard Medical School, which found that participants who practiced diaphragmatic breathing experienced significant reductions in stress and anxiety levels. They also reported improvements in their ability to concentrate and stay focused during tasks that demanded mental rigor—an essential quality for anyone preparing for exams.

To further illustrate, let's take John, an adult student who recently returned to school to pursue advanced certifications. Like many, he struggled with test anxiety which often impaired his performance. Upon learning about diaphragmatic breathing techniques, John began incorporating them into his daily regimen. He practiced every morning and evening, and before long, he noticed a marked improvement in his ability to remain calm and composed, particularly during exams. What once was an overwhelming experience transformed into a manageable task, thanks to the regular practice of diaphragmatic breathing.

The real beauty of this technique lies in its simplicity and accessibility. No special equipment or extensive time commitments are required—just your presence and willingness to breathe deeply. This practice empowers you to take charge of your well-being and effectively manage anxiety.

In conclusion, diaphragmatic breathing represents a vital tool in the arsenal against test anxiety. It offers a straightforward, scientifically-backed method to reduce stress, enhance mental clarity, and bolster confidence. By making diaphragmatic breathing an integral part of your daily life and utilizing it during exams, you create a supportive framework that can significantly improve your academic experience and performance. So take a deep breath, and embrace this practice to navigate the pressures of exams with greater ease and assurance.

Alternate Nostril Breathing

Alternate nostril breathing is a remarkably effective technique for balancing airflow and promoting a sense of equilibrium in the body. This practice, rooted in ancient yogic traditions, involves the intentional regulation of breath through one nostril at a time, which fosters a calming effect on the nervous system. By engaging in this simple yet profound exercise, you can stimulate the parasympathetic nervous response, thus reducing anxiety and facilitating a more tranquil state of mind.

Here is what you can do in order to achieve the goal:

- First, find a comfortable seated position with your spine straight but relaxed.
- Next, use your right thumb to softly close your right nostril and inhale deeply through your left nostril.
- Upon reaching a full inhalation, use your ring finger or pinky of the same hand to close your left nostril, then release your right nostril and exhale completely through it.
- After the exhalation, keep the left nostril closed, and inhale deeply through the right nostril.
- Close the right nostril again with your thumb and open the left nostril to exhale fully.

Repeat this cycle for several minutes. As you focus on your breath, you'll begin to notice a shift towards inner balance and tranquility.

Practicing alternate nostril breathing can notably quiet the mind and reduce racing thoughts, creating a centered state of awareness conducive to exam performance. The rhythm and focus required for this practice pull your attention away from anxious thoughts and ground you in the present moment. This technique offers a gentle, methodical approach to achieving mental calmness that can be particularly beneficial for those prone to pre-exam jitters.

The process itself acts as an anchor, drawing focus inward and cultivating mindfulness. Paying attention to each breath encourages disengagement from external stressors and internal distractions. This redirection of attention helps in diminishing the persistent cloud of anxiety that often precedes exams, allowing you to maintain a clearer, more organized thought process.

Incorporate alternate nostril breathing as a preparatory ritual before studying or taking exams to enhance cognitive function and reduce anxiety levels. Creating a routine around this practice can signal to your brain that it's time to shift into a mode of focused productivity. Over time, this consistency builds a positive association between the act of breathing and the onset of heightened mental clarity.

Engaging in this breathing exercise prior to study sessions primes your mind for absorbing and processing information efficiently. Likewise, employing it immediately before an exam can instill a sense of preparedness and composure, helping to counteract the adrenaline-fueled responses that can impede cognitive performance. This ritualistic aspect nurtures a habitual state of readiness and confidence, contributing to incremental improvements in academic performance.

Utilize alternate nostril breathing as a technique to ground oneself in the present moment, fostering a composed and focused mindset for optimal exam performance. Anxiety often pulls us either into ruminations about past failures or into the unknown of future outcomes. Grounding practices like this specific breathing exercise serve to anchor our minds firmly in the now, where we have agency and control.

By bringing your focus to the immediate experience of breathing, you effectively diminish the power of distracting thoughts and anxieties. This grounding creates a stable mental platform, allowing you to approach exams with a clear head and steady nerves. In essence, it cultivates a mental environment where productive thinking can flourish, free from the turmoil of extraneous stressors.

In summary, incorporating alternate nostril breathing into your routine can be a highly valuable tool for calming mental chatter, enhancing concentration, and promoting a state of calm readiness for exams. This method not only aids in alleviating immediate symptoms of anxiety but also establishes a structured pathway towards greater mental clarity and focus. Whether you are preparing for a significant professional certification or tackling an academic examination, adopting this practice can yield meaningful benefits in managing stress and optimizing performance.

As always, empirical evidence supports the efficacy of such techniques in reducing anxiety and improving cognitive functions. Studies indicate that regular practice of controlled breathing exercises positively influences physiological markers of stress, such as heart rate variability and cortisol levels. Therefore, embracing alternate nostril breathing not only serves as a practical strategy for immediate anxiety relief but also contributes to long-term mental well-being.

Remember, the objective is to integrate this practice seamlessly into your daily life, making it a natural and indispensable part of your preparation toolkit. Through consistent application, you'll discover that the seemingly simple act of conscious breathing holds profound potential to transform your exam experiences from sources of dread into opportunities for demonstrating your true capabilities.

Box Breathing Method

Box breathing, also known as square breathing, is a powerful technique designed to help manage anxiety and enhance focus during high-pressure situations, such as exams. This method involves a four-step pattern of inhaling, holding the breath, exhaling, and pausing before the next inhale, which together create a rectangular or box-like rhythm. Let's delve into how this technique can be applied effectively.

The essence of box breathing lies in its structured approach to controlling your breath. The process is simple yet remarkably effective:

- First, sit comfortably with your back straight and feet flat on the ground.

- Inhale slowly and deeply through your nose for a count of four.
- Hold your breath for another count of four.
- Exhale gently through your mouth for a count of four.
- Pause and hold your lungs empty for the final count of four before beginning the cycle again.

By engaging in this deliberate pattern, you intentionally regulate the nervous system. This practice increases oxygen flow to the brain, promoting mental alertness and helping stabilize your mood under stress. In the context of exam preparations, integrating box breathing into your routine can significantly reduce feelings of panic and overwhelm.

When you regularly practice box breathing, you train your body and mind to remain calm and collected. Not only does this act as a stabilizing force during study sessions, but it also serves as a reliable anchor during actual exams. The key here is consistency—make it a habit to practice box breathing every day, starting with just a few minutes and gradually increasing the duration as you become more comfortable with the technique.

Additionally, box breathing helps foster a deep awareness of your breath. This mindfulness aspect plays a crucial role in synchronizing the mind-body connection, bringing a sense of control over your emotions. By directing your focus inward and paying attention to the rhythm of your breathing, you shift your mental state from chaos to calmness. This heightened awareness allows you to respond to exam challenges with a composed and clear mindset, rather than reacting impulsively out of anxiety.

One of the greatest advantages of box breathing is its portability and discretion. You can practice it anytime, anywhere—whether you're sitting in the exam hall waiting for the papers to be distributed, or feeling a surge of nerves while answering questions. This method doesn't require any special equipment or space, making it an ideal tool for centering yourself in high-pressure environments. Moreover, because it's inconspicuous, you can employ it without drawing attention to yourself, further enhancing your ability to stay composed and confident during exams.

Incorporating box breathing into your exam preparation strategy can empower you to manage anxiety, enhance concentration, and approach each test with a sense of readiness and confidence. By mastering this technique, you build a solid foundation for handling stressful situations not only in academic settings but in various aspects of life.

To sum up, the box breathing method is a practical, evidence-based approach to managing test anxiety. Through regular practice, you can harness its benefits to regulate the nervous system, increase oxygen flow to the brain, and promote mental stability. As you gain proficiency in this technique, you'll find yourself better equipped to face exam challenges with a composed and confident mindset. Remember, persistence is key—dedicate time to practice box breathing daily, and soon it will become a natural part of your stress-management toolkit, ready to support you whenever the need arises.

Harnessing Breathing Techniques for Exam Success

Incorporating deep breathing techniques into your exam preparation routine offers a formidable solution to managing anxiety and fostering a stable, confident mindset. We began by exploring how deep breathing can activate the body's relaxation response, mitigating the physical symptoms of stress, such as rapid heart rate and muscle tension. By practicing slow, deliberate breaths, your nervous system transitions from a state of heightened alertness to one of calm repose, facilitating mental clarity and focus.

This chapter also discussed specific breathing methods like diaphragmatic breathing, alternate nostril breathing, and box breathing. Each technique provides a unique approach to regulating anxiety and enhancing overall well-being. Diaphragmatic breathing encourages full oxygenation of the body, promoting relaxation and reducing cortisol levels. Alternate nostril breathing cultivates balance within the nervous system, helping to quiet the mind and center your thoughts. Box breathing offers a structured rhythm that stabilizes mood and increases mental alertness under pressure.

Throughout this chapter, we underscored the importance of consistency in practice. Integrating these exercises into your daily routine—whether starting your day with a few minutes of focused breathing or using these techniques as quick resets during stressful moments—creates a foundation for resilience. This regular practice not only equips you to manage immediate stress but also builds long-term emotional stability, beneficial in many high-pressure scenarios beyond exams.

Nevertheless, it is important to recognize that while these techniques are highly effective, they require commitment and regular application. Some readers might feel overwhelmed by adding another task to their already busy schedules, yet the investment of time in these practices can yield significant dividends in reduced anxiety and improved performance. The broader implications of mastering these breathing techniques extend to various aspects of life, including professional settings and personal challenges, where maintaining composure under pressure is invaluable.

Ultimately, the value of these breathing exercises lies in their simplicity and accessibility. They empower you to take an active role in managing your stress, offering a sense of control when facing daunting situations. As you continue to hone these skills, you may find yourself better prepared not just for exams, but for any challenge that comes your way. The journey towards mastery begins with your next breath—take it deeply, and let it guide you towards greater confidence and peace of mind.

Chapter 5

Breathing Exercisesfor Test Confidence

The sound of your heart pounding in your chest, the shallow breaths that seem to quicken with every second, and the persistent flutter of nerves in your stomach—these are familiar sensations to anyone who has faced the pressure of an impending exam. Imagine having a simple tool at your disposal that could transform that tension into a sense of calm and control, one breath at a time. This chapter offers just that—a collection of breathing exercises designed to help you manage test anxiety and boost your confidence, allowing you to navigate exams with greater ease.

Exam stress is a common hurdle for adult students and professionals alike, often manifesting in both mental and physical symptoms. Think about the moments before an exam when your mind races through worst-case scenarios, or during the test itself when a challenging question triggers a wave of panic. These reactions can cloud your judgment, impair your focus, and ultimately affect your performance. For instance, Joe, a mid-career professional aspiring for certification, found himself paralyzed by these anxiety symptoms despite his extensive preparation. His experience isn't unique; many face similar struggles that undermine their true potential.

In this chapter, we will delve into various breathing techniques that can be seamlessly incorporated into your routine to mitigate these anxiety symptoms. From deep breathing to diaphragmatic methods and alternate nostril exercises, each technique is explained in detail, offering practical steps and the science behind how they work. You will discover strategies to implement these exercises both as part of your daily regimen and in high-pressure situations like exams. The goal is to equip you with tools to reclaim your peace of mind, enhance focus, and approach tests with newfound confidence.

Deep Breathing Techniques

It's no secret that exams can be a significant source of stress and anxiety for many adult students. Whether you're returning to school after years in the workforce or pursuing further certifications to advance your career, the pressure to perform well can feel overwhelming. One practical strategy to manage this stress effectively is through deep breathing exercises. These techniques not only help calm the mind and body but also instill a sense of control and confidence, crucial during high-stakes situations like exams.

Deep breathing involves a simple yet powerful process that activates the body's relaxation response. Here's how you can do it:

- **Inhale slowly through your nose** , allowing your abdomen to expand as you fill your lungs with air.
- **Hold your breath for a few seconds** , generally counting up to four or five.
- **Exhale gently through your mouth** , ensuring the exhale is slower than the inhale.

This method works by stimulating the parasympathetic nervous system, which counteracts the body's fight-or-flight response triggered by anxiety. By practicing this sequence, you can shift your physiological state from one of heightened alertness to one of calming repose.

In moments of acute stress, such as right before an exam or during a particularly challenging question, deep breathing can be a lifesaver. When anxiety strikes, it often manifests physically—your heart races, your muscles tense, and your breath becomes shallow and rapid. Engaging in deep breathing helps to recalibrate your nervous system, reducing these physical symptoms. This action creates a feedback loop where calming the body contributes to calming the mind, allowing you to regain focus and composure.

Here is what you can do in order to achieve the goal:

- **Pause** whatever you're doing at the first sign of mounting stress.
- **Focus on your breathing** by directing your attention inward. Start with a slow inhale through your nose.
- **Count silently as you hold your breath** —this small mental activity shifts focus away from anxiety-inducing thoughts.
- **Exhale slowly and completely** , emptying your lungs of all the air.
- Repeat the cycle a few times until you notice your heartbeat slowing and muscles relaxing.

What's more, these deep breathing techniques can be done discreetly in the exam room itself. Suppose you're mid-exam, feeling the pressure building up, find yourself a quiet moment to engage in a few cycles of deep breathing. The beauty of this practice lies in its subtlety; others around you won't even realize you're employing a coping mechanism. By managing your stress levels on the spot, you can maintain your focus and keep anxiety-induced errors at bay.

Furthermore, incorporating deep breathing into your daily routine can cultivate longer-term resilience against test anxiety. Regular practice trains your body to respond more calmly under pressure, creating a foundation of emotional stability. Consider integrating deep breathing exercises into your morning or evening routines.

Guidelines to incorporate deep breathing into your daily life:

- **Start your day** with a brief session of deep breathing. Just five minutes in the morning can set a positive tone for the rest of the day.
- **Take short breaks** throughout your day to practice deep breathing. These mini-sessions can serve as a quick reset during stressful periods.
- **End your day** with another round of deep breathing. This helps transition your mind and body into a relaxed state conducive to restful sleep.
- **Combine deep breathing with other relaxation techniques** like meditation or progressive muscle relaxation for enhanced benefits.

By making this a habit, you're essentially training your nervous system to remain balanced, even in stressful scenarios.

The consistent practice of these exercises fosters a reliable coping mechanism for anxiety, enhancing your overall sense of control during exams. It's like having an internal reset button that you can press anytime things start to feel overwhelming. Moreover, this learned skill extends beyond exams and can be utilized in various high-pressure situations, be it delivering a presentation at work or navigating personal challenges.

To sum up, deep breathing exercises offer a practical, evidence-based way to manage test anxiety. By learning to control your breathing, you can activate your body's natural relaxation response, calm your nervous system, and reduce the physical symptoms of anxiety. The ability to perform this technique discreetly in the exam room ensures you can maintain focus and control even when faced with difficult questions. And by implementing deep breathing into your daily routine, you build a resilience that not only aids in exam performance but also contributes to overall well-being.

Give it a try. The next time you feel the weight of exam stress pressing down, pause, breathe deeply, and reclaim your peace of mind. You may find that this simple technique not only improves your performance but also leaves you feeling more empowered and confident in the face of challenges.

Diaphragmatic Breathing Techniques

Diaphragmatic breathing involves breathing deeply into the abdomen, expanding the diaphragm to fully oxygenate the body and release tension. This technique is widely recognized in both scientific literature and clinical practice as an effective method for reducing anxiety and promoting relaxation. Here's how you can implement this practice to help manage stress and maintain composure during exams:

- **Find a quiet place** where you won't be disturbed for a few minutes.
- **Sit or lie down comfortably** , ensuring your back is straight if sitting.
- **Place one hand on your chest and the other on your abdomen** , just below your rib cage.
- **Inhale slowly through your nose** , allowing your abdomen (not your chest) to rise as you fill your lungs with air.
- **Exhale gently through your mouth** , letting the air flow out naturally while feeling your abdomen fall.

Practicing diaphragmatic breathing exercises regularly trains the body to respond calmly to stressors and maintain focus under pressure. It's important to integrate this practice into your daily routine so it becomes second nature. By doing so, you can condition your body to activate this relaxation response automatically in stressful situations, such as taking exams or dealing with unexpected challenges.

Regular practice doesn't have to be time-consuming. You can incorporate short sessions of diaphragmatic breathing into your day. Start with a few minutes each morning and evening, gradually increasing the duration as you become more comfortable. Over time, your body will learn to adopt this calmer state more quickly and efficiently.

Adopting diaphragmatic breathing as a tool to center oneself before exams can promote a sense of calm and confidence in one's abilities. When you face the exam room's intimidating environment, a brief session of focused breathing can help anchor your mind and body. Taking a few deep, controlled breaths can signal your nervous system to de-escalate any rising tension, creating a mental space where you feel more in control and less prone to anxiety.

Utilizing diaphragmatic breathing as a quick and effective way to manage test anxiety symptoms and maintain a clear mindset during exams is practical and accessible. In the midst of an exam, you might encounter moments where nerves spike and clarity fades. A swift return to diaphragmatic breathing can act as a reset button, helping you regain focus and proceed with greater ease.

In essence, diaphragmatic breathing is a powerful technique for individuals to relax their body and mind, fostering a conducive environment for exam success and confidence. This simple yet effective method can empower you to take control of your physiological responses to stress, ensuring that anxiety does not overshadow your preparation and performance. By integrating this practice into your routine and utilizing it during crucial moments, you set the groundwork for a calmer, more confident approach to exams.

Understanding the mechanics and benefits of diaphragmatic breathing provides a foundation, but the true effectiveness lies in consistent practice. The more you engage in these exercises, the more ingrained they become, offering reliable support in times of need. It's about building a habit that aligns with your physiological need for balance and calm, especially when facing high-pressure scenarios like exams.

Moreover, research supports the efficacy of diaphragmatic breathing in reducing symptoms of anxiety and improving overall well-being. Studies have shown that those who practice this form of breathing regularly exhibit lower levels of cortisol, the stress hormone, and increased activity in parts of the brain associated with emotional regulation and cognitive function.

Consider, for instance, a study conducted by Harvard Medical School, which found that participants who practiced diaphragmatic breathing experienced significant reductions in stress and anxiety levels. They also reported improvements in their ability to concentrate and stay focused during tasks that demanded mental rigor—an essential quality for anyone preparing for exams.

To further illustrate, let's take John, an adult student who recently returned to school to pursue advanced certifications. Like many, he struggled with test anxiety which often impaired his performance. Upon learning about diaphragmatic breathing techniques, John began incorporating them into his daily regimen. He practiced every morning and evening, and before long, he noticed a marked improvement in his ability to remain calm and composed, particularly during exams. What once was an overwhelming experience transformed into a manageable task, thanks to the regular practice of diaphragmatic breathing.

The real beauty of this technique lies in its simplicity and accessibility. No special equipment or extensive time commitments are required—just your presence and willingness to breathe deeply. This practice empowers you to take charge of your well-being and effectively manage anxiety.

In conclusion, diaphragmatic breathing represents a vital tool in the arsenal against test anxiety. It offers a straightforward, scientifically-backed method to reduce stress, enhance mental clarity, and bolster confidence. By making diaphragmatic breathing an integral part of your daily life and utilizing it during exams, you create a supportive framework that can significantly improve your academic experience and performance. So take a deep breath, and embrace this practice to navigate the pressures of exams with greater ease and assurance.

Alternate Nostril Breathing

Alternate nostril breathing is a remarkably effective technique for balancing airflow and promoting a sense of equilibrium in the body. This practice, rooted in ancient yogic traditions, involves the intentional regulation of breath through one nostril at a time, which fosters a calming effect on the nervous system. By engaging in this simple yet profound exercise, you can stimulate the parasympathetic nervous response, thus reducing anxiety and facilitating a more tranquil state of mind.

Here is what you can do in order to achieve the goal:

- First, find a comfortable seated position with your spine straight but relaxed.
- Next, use your right thumb to softly close your right nostril and inhale deeply through your left nostril.
- Upon reaching a full inhalation, use your ring finger or pinky of the same hand to close your left nostril, then release your right nostril and exhale completely through it.
- After the exhalation, keep the left nostril closed, and inhale deeply through the right nostril.
- Close the right nostril again with your thumb and open the left nostril to exhale fully.

Repeat this cycle for several minutes. As you focus on your breath, you'll begin to notice a shift towards inner balance and tranquility.

Practicing alternate nostril breathing can notably quiet the mind and reduce racing thoughts, creating a centered state of awareness conducive to exam performance. The rhythm and focus required for this practice pull your attention away from anxious thoughts and ground you in the present moment. This technique offers a gentle, methodical approach to achieving mental calmness that can be particularly beneficial for those prone to pre-exam jitters.

The process itself acts as an anchor, drawing focus inward and cultivating mindfulness. Paying attention to each breath encourages disengagement from external stressors and internal distractions. This redirection of attention helps in diminishing the persistent cloud of anxiety that often precedes exams, allowing you to maintain a clearer, more organized thought process.

Incorporate alternate nostril breathing as a preparatory ritual before studying or taking exams to enhance cognitive function and reduce anxiety levels. Creating a routine around this practice can signal to your brain that it's time to shift into a mode of focused productivity. Over time, this consistency builds a positive association between the act of breathing and the onset of heightened mental clarity.

Engaging in this breathing exercise prior to study sessions primes your mind for absorbing and processing information efficiently. Likewise, employing it immediately before an exam can instill a sense of preparedness and composure, helping to counteract the adrenaline-fueled responses that can impede cognitive performance. This ritualistic aspect nurtures a habitual state of readiness and confidence, contributing to incremental improvements in academic performance.

Utilize alternate nostril breathing as a technique to ground oneself in the present moment, fostering a composed and focused mindset for optimal exam performance. Anxiety often pulls us either into ruminations about past failures or into the unknown of future outcomes. Grounding practices like this specific breathing exercise serve to anchor our minds firmly in the now, where we have agency and control.

By bringing your focus to the immediate experience of breathing, you effectively diminish the power of distracting thoughts and anxieties. This grounding creates a stable mental platform, allowing you to approach exams with a clear head and steady nerves. In essence, it cultivates a mental environment where productive thinking can flourish, free from the turmoil of extraneous stressors.

In summary, incorporating alternate nostril breathing into your routine can be a highly valuable tool for calming mental chatter, enhancing concentration, and promoting a state of calm readiness for exams. This method not only aids in alleviating immediate symptoms of anxiety but also establishes a structured pathway towards greater mental clarity and focus. Whether you are preparing for a significant professional certification or tackling an academic examination, adopting this practice can yield meaningful benefits in managing stress and optimizing performance.

As always, empirical evidence supports the efficacy of such techniques in reducing anxiety and improving cognitive functions. Studies indicate that regular practice of controlled breathing exercises positively influences physiological markers of stress, such as heart rate variability and cortisol levels. Therefore, embracing alternate nostril breathing not only serves as a practical strategy for immediate anxiety relief but also contributes to long-term mental well-being.

Remember, the objective is to integrate this practice seamlessly into your daily life, making it a natural and indispensable part of your preparation toolkit. Through consistent application, you'll discover that the seemingly simple act of conscious breathing holds profound potential to transform your exam experiences from sources of dread into opportunities for demonstrating your true capabilities.

Box Breathing Method

Box breathing, also known as square breathing, is a powerful technique designed to help manage anxiety and enhance focus during high-pressure situations, such as exams. This method involves a four-step pattern of inhaling, holding the breath, exhaling, and pausing before the next inhale, which together create a rectangular or box-like rhythm. Let's delve into how this technique can be applied effectively.

The essence of box breathing lies in its structured approach to controlling your breath. The process is simple yet remarkably effective:

- First, sit comfortably with your back straight and feet flat on the ground.

- Inhale slowly and deeply through your nose for a count of four.
- Hold your breath for another count of four.
- Exhale gently through your mouth for a count of four.
- Pause and hold your lungs empty for the final count of four before beginning the cycle again.

By engaging in this deliberate pattern, you intentionally regulate the nervous system. This practice increases oxygen flow to the brain, promoting mental alertness and helping stabilize your mood under stress. In the context of exam preparations, integrating box breathing into your routine can significantly reduce feelings of panic and overwhelm.

When you regularly practice box breathing, you train your body and mind to remain calm and collected. Not only does this act as a stabilizing force during study sessions, but it also serves as a reliable anchor during actual exams. The key here is consistency—make it a habit to practice box breathing every day, starting with just a few minutes and gradually increasing the duration as you become more comfortable with the technique.

Additionally, box breathing helps foster a deep awareness of your breath. This mindfulness aspect plays a crucial role in synchronizing the mind-body connection, bringing a sense of control over your emotions. By directing your focus inward and paying attention to the rhythm of your breathing, you shift your mental state from chaos to calmness. This heightened awareness allows you to respond to exam challenges with a composed and clear mindset, rather than reacting impulsively out of anxiety.

One of the greatest advantages of box breathing is its portability and discretion. You can practice it anytime, anywhere—whether you're sitting in the exam hall waiting for the papers to be distributed, or feeling a surge of nerves while answering questions. This method doesn't require any special equipment or space, making it an ideal tool for centering yourself in high-pressure environments. Moreover, because it's inconspicuous, you can employ it without drawing attention to yourself, further enhancing your ability to stay composed and confident during exams.

Incorporating box breathing into your exam preparation strategy can empower you to manage anxiety, enhance concentration, and approach each test with a sense of readiness and confidence. By mastering this technique, you build a solid foundation for handling stressful situations not only in academic settings but in various aspects of life.

To sum up, the box breathing method is a practical, evidence-based approach to managing test anxiety. Through regular practice, you can harness its benefits to regulate the nervous system, increase oxygen flow to the brain, and promote mental stability. As you gain proficiency in this technique, you'll find yourself better equipped to face exam challenges with a composed and confident mindset. Remember, persistence is key—dedicate time to practice box breathing daily, and soon it will become a natural part of your stress-management toolkit, ready to support you whenever the need arises.

Harnessing Breathing Techniques for Exam Success

Incorporating deep breathing techniques into your exam preparation routine offers a formidable solution to managing anxiety and fostering a stable, confident mindset. We began by exploring how deep breathing can activate the body's relaxation response, mitigating the physical symptoms of stress, such as rapid heart rate and muscle tension. By practicing slow, deliberate breaths, your nervous system transitions from a state of heightened alertness to one of calm repose, facilitating mental clarity and focus.

This chapter also discussed specific breathing methods like diaphragmatic breathing, alternate nostril breathing, and box breathing. Each technique provides a unique approach to regulating anxiety and enhancing overall well-being. Diaphragmatic breathing encourages full oxygenation of the body, promoting relaxation and reducing cortisol levels. Alternate nostril breathing cultivates balance within the nervous system, helping to quiet the mind and center your thoughts. Box breathing offers a structured rhythm that stabilizes mood and increases mental alertness under pressure.

Throughout this chapter, we underscored the importance of consistency in practice. Integrating these exercises into your daily routine—whether starting your day with a few minutes of focused breathing or using these techniques as quick resets during stressful moments—creates a foundation for resilience. This regular practice not only equips you to manage immediate stress but also builds long-term emotional stability, beneficial in many high-pressure scenarios beyond exams.

Nevertheless, it is important to recognize that while these techniques are highly effective, they require commitment and regular application. Some readers might feel overwhelmed by adding another task to their already busy schedules, yet the investment of time in these practices can yield significant dividends in reduced anxiety and improved performance. The broader implications of mastering these breathing techniques extend to various aspects of life, including professional settings and personal challenges, where maintaining composure under pressure is invaluable.

Ultimately, the value of these breathing exercises lies in their simplicity and accessibility. They empower you to take an active role in managing your stress, offering a sense of control when facing daunting situations. As you continue to hone these skills, you may find yourself better prepared not just for exams, but for any challenge that comes your way. The journey towards mastery begins with your next breath—take it deeply, and let it guide you towards greater confidence and peace of mind.

Chapter 6

Overcoming Perfectionism in Academic Settings

Perfectionism in academic settings can appear deceptively beneficial at first glance. Many adult students and professionals pursuing further education hold themselves to lofty standards, believing this will lead to unrivaled success. Yet, the relentless pursuit of flawlessness often yields diminishing returns, leading not to higher grades or better performance, but to anxiety, burnout, and hindered progress. The drive for perfection can become an invisible adversary, subtly undermining efforts and well-being.

The problems associated with perfectionistic tendencies are multifaceted. For instance, the fear of making mistakes can result in procrastination as students delay tasks to avoid potential errors. This delays productive engagement and reinforces a cycle of stress and self-doubt. Additionally, setting unattainable goals creates a scenario where any achievement short of perfection feels like a failure, exacerbating feelings of inadequacy and reducing overall motivation. Imagine a student who spends countless hours perfecting every detail of an assignment, only to find that their exhaustive efforts leave them no time for other essential study activities. Such scenarios highlight how perfectionism, instead of pushing one towards excellence, often results in counterproductive outcomes.

In this chapter, we will delve into practical strategies for overcoming perfectionism by addressing these tendencies head-on and learning to set more realistic, achievable goals. We will explore methods to reframe objectives, making them manageable and less intimidating. Furthermore, we will discuss techniques for embracing imperfection and viewing mistakes as integral components of the learning process. By shifting focus from unrealistic standards to steady progress, students can alleviate performance pressure and cultivate a healthier, more balanced approach to their academic pursuits.

Understanding the Negative Impact of Perfectionism on Exam Performance

Addressing perfectionistic tendencies and setting realistic goals is crucial for alleviating performance pressure and anxiety. As adult students preparing for exams or professionals pursuing further education, understanding how to navigate these challenges effectively can significantly enhance both academic performance and personal well-being.

Let's delve into the crux of perfectionism's impact on exam performance. Perfectionism often masquerades as a motivator, pushing you to aim higher and work harder. However, it frequently results in heightened anxiety and self-imposed pressure. This stress doesn't just affect your mental health; it actively hinders your ability to perform at your best. When every task must be flawless, the fear of making mistakes can paralyze you, leading to procrastination or burnout. It is critical to recognize that striving for unattainable standards sets you up for failure, both psychologically and academically.

Recognizing unrealistic standards and expectations is the first step toward setting more attainable and healthier goals. Often, we impose these high standards on ourselves without pausing to consider their feasibility. Here is what you can do to set attainable goals:

- Start by identifying specific areas where your standards are highest.

- Reflect on whether these standards stem from external pressures or internal aspirations.

- Reframe your objectives to focus on progress rather than perfection.
- Break larger tasks into smaller, manageable steps and celebrate each milestone reached.

By doing this, you can alleviate some of the undue stress and create a path that is easier to follow, reducing the overall pressure you feel.

Embracing the concept of 'good enough' is another powerful strategy. Letting go of the need for everything to be perfect opens the door to greater focus and productivity. Often, the pursuit of perfection can consume valuable time and energy that could be better spent on other tasks. By accepting 'good enough,' you allow yourself to move forward without the constant burden of trying to achieve the unachievable. Here's how you can get started:

- Set clear, realistic expectations for your tasks and assignments.
- Allow room for imperfection and understand that it doesn't equate to failure.
- Allocate a specific amount of time to tasks and stick to it, avoiding overworking for marginal gains.
- Practice self-compassion by acknowledging your efforts and improvements rather than fixating on flaws.

This approach helps to build a sustainable study routine, ensuring that you remain productive without burning out.

Another key element is accepting mistakes as part of the learning process. Making errors is inevitable and intrinsic to growth and development. Viewing mistakes not as failures but as opportunities to learn can profoundly improve your resilience and approach to academic challenges. Here are some guidelines to foster this mindset:

- Reflect on past mistakes to identify what went wrong and what you learned.
- Incorporate regular review sessions to assess your progress and adapt your strategies.
- Embrace feedback as a tool for improvement rather than criticism.
- Cultivate a growth mindset where you view setbacks as temporary and surmountable.

Incorporating these elements into your study habits can turn perceived weaknesses into strengths, enabling you to approach exams with a clearer mind and a more resilient attitude.

A core takeaway from all these strategies is to embrace progress over perfection. Life and academics are marathons, not sprints. Prioritize ongoing learning and steady improvement over flawless outcomes. This doesn't mean lowering your standards but rather adjusting them to be more inclusive of human fallibility and the natural learning curve.

In the context of adult learners and professionals, balancing these factors might seem challenging amidst existing responsibilities. However, integrating these practices into daily routines can help manage performance anxiety more effectively. Whether it's through setting achievable goals, allowing 'good enough' to be sufficient, or learning from mistakes, each action fosters a more balanced and less stressful approach to exams and continuous education.

Moreover, balancing economic growth and human welfare forms the larger framework within which these personal strategies operate. By ensuring human welfare takes precedence, you lay the groundwork for a healthier, more equitable society. Your individual success contributes to this collective goal, emphasizing personal responsibility while advocating for necessary safety nets.

Combining personal freedom with social responsibility means recognizing that while you're striving for personal excellence, contributing to a supportive and compassionate community also holds value. This dual focus can alleviate some of the isolation and pressure that comes with perfectionism, reminding you that it's okay to rely on others and offer support in return.

Finally, let's reflect on checks and balances. Just as government and corporations should work together under careful scrutiny to protect public interests, so should you balance your ambitions with realistic self-care. Self-imposed rules and societal expectations should serve to elevate your wellbeing, not undermine it.

Remember, tackling perfectionism and setting realistic goals is not about lowering your standards but about aligning them with what is achievable and healthy. It's about embracing a holistic view where progress, learning, and self-compassion take center stage. Striving for meaningful goals that prioritize your welfare will ultimately lead you to more fulfilling achievements, both academically and personally.

In sum, addressing perfectionistic tendencies involves recognizing and adjusting unrealistic standards, embracing 'good enough,' accepting mistakes, and prioritizing steady progress. These strategies help create a balanced approach to exams and lifelong learning, mitigating anxiety and enhancing overall performance. As you continue to navigate your educational journey, remember that seeking improvement, staying resilient, and maintaining balance will serve you far better than chasing perfection ever could.

Setting Achievable Academic Goals and Expectations

Establishing realistic short-term and long-term goals can provide a sense of direction and accomplishment without overwhelming pressure. It's critical to remember that setting achievable academic goals is not about lowering your standards but about creating a sustainable path to success. When outlining your objectives, consider both immediate and future aspirations. Short-term goals might involve completing daily or weekly study tasks, while long-term goals could entail earning a degree or passing a certification exam.

Here is what you can do in order to achieve the goal:

- Start by clearly defining what you want to achieve. Write down your goals and make them as specific as possible.
- Break down each goal into smaller, manageable tasks. This map will guide you through the process step-by-step, making the larger goal feel less daunting.
- Assign deadlines to these smaller tasks. This helps to maintain momentum and provides regular checkpoints to assess your progress.
- Periodically review and adjust your goals if necessary. Life is unpredictable, and being flexible with your plans ensures you stay on track without feeling overwhelmed.

Breaking down larger tasks into manageable steps can make academic pursuits more achievable and less daunting. Think of this as using stepping stones to cross a wide river. Each small step brings you closer to the other side without the risk of falling in. For instance, instead of attempting to study an entire textbook in one sitting, break it down into chapters or sections and focus on understanding one part at a time.

Creating a balanced study schedule that allows for adequate preparation and self-care can enhance productivity and well-being. A balanced schedule doesn't mean cramming every free minute with study time; it means allocating time wisely between academics, rest, and leisure. The key is consistency over intensity. Devote dedicated hours each day to studying, but also prioritize breaks, physical activity, and social interactions.

Here is what you can do in order to achieve the goal:

- Design a daily or weekly timetable that includes all your commitments. Use tools like calendars or study planners to organize your time effectively.
- Ensure you allocate specific time blocks exclusively for study sessions. Treat these times as non-negotiable appointments with yourself.
- Integrate short breaks between study periods. Techniques such as the Pomodoro Technique, where you work for 25 minutes and then break for 5 minutes, can be particularly effective.

- Don't forget to schedule downtime. Activities like exercise, hobbies, or simply relaxing are crucial for maintaining mental and physical health.

Seeking feedback and guidance from educators or mentors can help in adjusting goals and expectations for academic success. It's vital to understand that academic growth isn't a solitary journey. Support systems exist to guide you and offer valuable insights. Educators, tutors, and mentors possess years of experience and knowledge. They can provide personalized advice that aligns with your strengths and areas for improvement.

Here is what you can do in order to achieve the goal:

- Initiate regular check-ins with your educators or mentors. Discuss your progress, challenges, and any adjustments needed in your approach.

- Actively seek constructive feedback on assignments or practice exams. Understanding mistakes and learning from them is an essential part of growth.

- Utilize office hours or set appointments for one-on-one discussions. This personalized attention can clarify doubts and strengthen your understanding.

- Don't hesitate to ask questions. No query is too small, and curiosity often leads to deeper comprehension and innovation.

Focusing on progress rather than perfection is a mindset shift that significantly alleviates performance pressure and anxiety. Perfectionism can create unrealistic standards that are impossible to meet, leading to constant stress and disappointment. Instead, celebrate small victories and recognize incremental improvements. This positive reinforcement builds confidence and motivation over time.

For example, if your goal was to read three chapters this week but you only managed two, acknowledge the effort you put in rather than beating yourself up for not finishing the third. Each step forward, no matter how small, is still progress.

Here is what you can do in order to make this shift:

- Set process-based goals rather than outcome-based goals. Focus on the efforts you put into studying, not just the grades you receive.

- Maintain a journal to track your achievements and reflect on your learning journey. Writing about what you've accomplished can reinforce a sense of progress.

- Create a reward system for meeting milestones. Small rewards can serve as incentives and boost your morale.

- Practice self-compassion. Remind yourself that everyone has ups and downs, and setbacks are part of the learning process.

Lastly, seeking support when needed is crucial to maintaining motivation and goal clarity. Recognize when you're struggling and don't shy away from asking for help. Whether it's friends, family, mental health professionals, or academic advisors, tapping into your support network can provide different perspectives, encouragement, and practical assistance.

Here is what you can do in order to seek support:

- Reach out to peers for group study sessions. Collaborative learning can enhance understanding and make studying more enjoyable.

- Join academic support groups or online forums where you can share experiences and gain insights from others facing similar challenges.

- Consider speaking to a counselor or therapist if stress and anxiety become overwhelming. Professional guidance can offer strategies for managing mental health effectively.

- Build a support system that includes individuals who uplift and inspire you. Surrounding yourself with positive influences fosters a conducive environment for success.

In summary, setting realistic goals, breaking tasks into manageable steps, balancing study and self-care, seeking feedback, focusing on progress, and getting support are foundational strategies for alleviating performance pressure and enhancing academic success. By embracing these principles, you can navigate the academic landscape with confidence and resilience, turning potential stressors into opportunities for growth. Remember, your journey isn't just about reaching a destination—it's about appreciating and learning from every step along the way.

Embracing Imperfection and Learning from Mistakes

Embracing imperfection and learning from mistakes

We live in a society that often holds perfection up as the ultimate goal, especially in academic settings. However, this pursuit of perfection can lead to paralyzing anxiety and performance pressure, neither of which are conducive to genuine learning or personal growth. Embracing imperfection and viewing mistakes as opportunities for growth and improvement can significantly shift our perspective from seeing failure as a setback to recognizing it as a stepping stone.

When you make a mistake on an exam or experience a setback in your studies, it's easy to fall into self-criticism. But consider this: each error is not a confirmation of inadequacy, but rather an indicator of where there's room to grow. This shift in perspective does wonders for alleviating performance pressure. Instead of dreading exams for fear of making mistakes, you'll begin to see them as valuable feedback sessions.

Practicing self-compassion and self-forgiveness is pivotal in developing this positive outlook. When confronted with setbacks, it's essential to engage in positive self-talk. Here's a method you can use:

- Start by acknowledging your feelings without judgment. If you feel disappointed or stressed, recognize these emotions as valid.

- Then, remind yourself that everyone makes mistakes—all humans are fallible.

- Next, focus on what you've learned from the experience. Instead of zeroing in on what went wrong, reflect on what can be done better next time.

By adopting this mindset, you cultivate a supportive inner dialogue that can buffer the emotional impact of academic challenges. Remember, the way you talk to yourself matters immensely; it shapes your reality. Being kind to yourself doesn't mean avoiding accountability—it means treating yourself with the same empathy you would offer a friend who's facing similar struggles.

Engaging in reflective practices allows you to identify areas for development and implement strategies for future enhancement. Taking some time after each academic challenge to analyze what worked well and what didn't can provide actionable insights. Here's how you can conduct a reflective practice:

- Set aside quiet time to reflect on your recent experiences.

- Write down specific instances where you felt challenged or made mistakes.

- Reflect on the circumstances surrounding these instances. Were there external factors at play?

- Identify patterns in your challenges—are there recurring issues?

- Develop a plan to address these areas. What resources or strategies could help you improve?

Incorporating these reflections regularly builds a habit of continuous improvement. It also demystifies the process of learning, showing that growth is an ongoing journey rather than a fixed destination.

Embracing imperfection as a natural part of the learning journey can substantially reduce the fear of failure and increase resilience. Acknowledge that learning isn't linear; it comes with ups and downs.

Viewing imperfections as normal and expected parts of your educational path will help reduce the anxiety associated with performing flawlessly.

Let's break this down further:

- Understand that no one is infallible. Even experts and professionals were once beginners who made countless mistakes along their journey.
- Allow yourself to experiment without the fear of getting it wrong. When you approach tasks with curiosity instead of dread, you'll find more joy in the learning process.
- Celebrate small victories. Every step forward, no matter how minor, is progress. Recognize and appreciate these moments.

In doing so, you not only build resilience but also cultivate a broader perspective on what it means to succeed academically. Success isn't just about acing tests; it's about growing, adapting, and continuously refining your skills and knowledge.

To summarize the key takeaways: Embrace imperfection as a stepping stone to progress, cultivate self-compassion amidst difficulties, and use mistakes as opportunities for personal and academic growth. These practices will not only alleviate pressure but also create a more fulfilling and enriching educational experience.

Addressing perfectionistic tendencies and setting realistic goals is integral to managing performance pressure effectively. Many adult students preparing for academic exams may wrestle with high expectations they've set for themselves, leading to undue stress. It's crucial to set realistic goals that are both challenging and attainable. Here's how to do it:

- Begin by assessing your current capabilities and workload. Be honest about what you can manage within the available time.
- Break larger tasks into smaller, more manageable milestones. This makes overwhelming projects seem more achievable and less intimidating.
- Schedule regular reviews to assess your progress. Adjust your goals if necessary to remain aligned with your evolving understanding and skills.
- Celebrate each milestone. Recognizing achievements reinforces motivation and reduces the psychological burden of the overarching goal.

This balanced approach ensures that while you push yourself towards excellence, you do so sustainably and with kindness toward yourself.

In conclusion, by embracing imperfection, practicing self-compassion, engaging in reflective practices, and setting realistic goals, you equip yourself with the tools needed to convert anxiety into constructive energy. The journey of learning becomes less about avoiding mistakes and more about continuously evolving and improving. As you prepare for your academic exams, remember that true mastery lies not in the absence of mistakes but in the ability to learn from them and keep moving forward.

Developing Self-Compassion and Self-Acceptance

Developing self-compassion and self-acceptance in the pursuit of academic excellence involves a multifaceted approach. It's crucial to incorporate practices that foster mindfulness and self-awareness. By taking these steps, you can identify and challenge those pervasive self-critical thoughts that often accompany academic performance pressure.

Here is what you can do in order to achieve this:

- Start by setting aside a few minutes each day for mindfulness meditation. This practice can help you become more aware of your thoughts and emotions without immediate judgment.

- Journaling can be another effective tool. Reflect on your day, noting instances where self-critical thoughts came up. Over time, you'll begin to see patterns and triggers.

- Engage in reflective practices such as deep breathing exercises or yoga. These activities not only promote physical relaxation but also help in grounding your mind, making it easier to manage stress and anxiety.

Cultivating a sense of self-worth beyond academic achievements is paramount for fostering resilience and overall well-being. It can be easy to tie your self-esteem strictly to your grades or test scores, but it's essential to recognize your value outside of these metrics. Here are some guidelines to help you begin:

- Identify and celebrate your strengths and achievements in areas other than academics. Whether it's a hobby you're passionate about or an act of kindness you performed, acknowledging these moments can help shift your focus away from purely academic validation.

- Surround yourself with supportive friends and family members who appreciate you for who you are, not just what you achieve academically. Their perspective can reinforce the idea that your worth extends beyond your educational accomplishments.

- Practice positive self-talk. When you find yourself being overly critical, consciously counter those thoughts with affirmations and reminders of your intrinsic value.

Engaging in self-care practices and activities that promote emotional balance and stress reduction is another key component. Self-care isn't a luxury; it's a necessity, especially during periods of intense academic pressure.

Here is what you can do in order to achieve this:

- Exercise regularly. Physical activity has been proven to reduce stress and increase mental clarity. Whether it's a brisk walk or a rigorous workout, moving your body can make a significant difference.

- Ensure you get adequate sleep. Poor sleep can exacerbate anxiety and hamper cognitive function. Create a bedtime routine that helps you relax and wind down before sleeping.

- Incorporate enjoyable activities into your daily routine. Whether it's reading a book, playing a musical instrument, or spending time with loved ones, these activities can provide much-needed respite.

- Practice mindful eating. Paying attention to what you consume and how it makes you feel can have a profound impact on your overall well-being.

Seeking professional support or guidance when perfectionism impacts overall well-being is not only wise but often necessary. Sometimes, despite our best efforts, we need external support to navigate the challenges of perfectionism and performance anxiety.

Here is what you can do in order to achieve this:

- Consider speaking with a therapist or counselor who specializes in perfectionism and academic stress. They can provide tailored strategies to manage these tendencies.

- Look into support groups where you can connect with others facing similar struggles. Sharing experiences and coping mechanisms can be incredibly validating and helpful.

- Utilize campus resources if you're a student. Many educational institutions offer mental health services and workshops geared towards managing academic pressure.

- Don't hesitate to seek medical advice if anxiety is significantly affecting your daily life. Sometimes, medication or structured therapies like Cognitive Behavioral Therapy (CBT) can be beneficial.

Prioritizing self-care and mental health over academic achievements is not just about better performance; it's about sustainable success and overall life satisfaction. Remember, personal growth and well-being are far more important than external validation. By practicing self-compassion in moments of self-doubt or criticism, you build a foundation for a healthier, more balanced approach to academics and life in general.

Ultimately, these practices form a holistic strategy to address perfectionistic tendencies and alleviate the associated pressures and anxieties. The path to academic success does not solely depend on rigorous studying and high grades. Instead, it's equally dependent on nurturing your mental and emotional health, accepting your limitations, and recognizing that perfection is an unrealistic standard. Balancing these aspects will not only enhance your academic performance but also contribute to a richer, more fulfilling life.

In closing, remember that self-compassion is a learned skill, one that requires patience and persistent effort. By making small, deliberate changes in how you treat yourself, you pave the way for significant improvements in both your academic journey and overall well-being. Keep in mind that every step you take towards self-compassion and self-acceptance is a step towards a healthier, more resilient you.

Cultivating a Healthier Academic Mindset

In this chapter, we have delved into the importance of addressing perfectionistic tendencies and setting realistic goals as fundamental strategies to alleviate performance pressure and anxiety. Recognizing the negative impact that perfectionism can have on exam performance is the first step toward creating a healthier and more productive academic environment.

Returning to our earlier discussion, we noted that perfectionism often masquerades as a motivator but typically results in heightened anxiety and self-imposed pressure. This cycle of stress can paralyze you and hinder your ability to perform at your best. Our current position emphasizes that striving for unattainable standards does more harm than good.

Some readers might be concerned that setting more achievable goals means lowering their standards or settling for mediocrity. However, it is essential to understand that this approach is about aligning expectations with what is realistically attainable and maintaining well-being. The consequences of ignoring these principles are significant—continued pursuit of perfection can lead to chronic stress, burnout, and diminished academic performance.

On a broader scale, embracing realistic goals and learning from mistakes fosters a more compassionate and resilient approach to both academics and life. As individuals adopt these practices, they contribute to a culture that values progress over perfection, creating a supportive and inclusive community. This shift not only benefits personal development but also enhances collective academic excellence.

As we conclude this chapter, consider the notion that true success lies not in the absence of mistakes but in the ability to learn from them and continue evolving. Perfection is an unrealistic standard that can stifle growth. Instead, focus on steady progress, self-compassion, and resilience. By doing so, you pave the way for a fulfilling academic journey characterized by continuous improvement and balanced well-being.

In summary, tackling perfectionistic tendencies requires recognizing and adjusting unrealistic standards, embracing 'good enough,' accepting mistakes, and prioritizing steady progress. These strategies help create a balanced approach to exams and lifelong learning, mitigating anxiety and enhancing overall performance. Reflect on these principles as you navigate your academic path, reminding yourself that seeking improvement and maintaining balance will serve you far better than chasing perfection ever could.

Chapter 7

Building Exam Confidencethrough Positive Psychology

Exam settings often elicit a range of emotions, from nervousness to outright dread. The psychological pressure can be overwhelming, especially for adult students juggling various responsibilities or professionals aiming to advance their careers through certifications. Imagine walking into an exam room not with apprehension but with a calm sense of assurance, rooted in the knowledge that you have the skills and mindset necessary to succeed. This chapter delves into how principles of positive psychology can help achieve this sense of exam confidence.

Many individuals preparing for exams focus on their shortcomings, amplifying feelings of inadequacy and anxiety. It's common to hear internal monologues like, "I don't have enough time to study," or "I'm just not good at this subject." These negative thought patterns can be paralyzing and counterproductive. For instance, a working professional might feel overwhelmed by the dual pressures of job responsibilities and exam preparation, perceiving every mistake as evidence of impending failure. Such stress can erode self-esteem and make exam preparation even more daunting. By shifting the focus from limitations to possibilities, one can transform this negative cycle.

This chapter explores practical strategies like practicing gratitude and positive affirmations, which can shift your mental focus towards recognizing strengths and opportunities. Additionally, techniques such as visualizing success and reflecting on past achievements can reinforce a positive self-image, essential for building exam confidence. By engaging in these practices consistently, you create a mental framework that supports resilience and optimism. This chapter also highlights the benefits of cultivating a growth mindset, encouraging readers to view setbacks as avenues for improvement rather than as insurmountable obstacles. Together, these tools form a comprehensive approach to managing test anxiety, equipping you to face exams with newfound confidence and poise.

Practicing Gratitude and Positive Affirmations

Expressing gratitude for strengths and opportunities can shift the focus from limitations to possibilities. This principle has a solid grounding in evidence-based research and is extremely relevant when dealing with exam anxiety. Practicing gratitude involves acknowledging not only what we have but also recognizing our own abilities, resources, and support systems. For many adult students returning to education or pursuing further certifications, it's common to focus on what they lack—time, perhaps, or certain skills—thereby amplifying stress.

Engaging in an intentional gratitude practice can help transform this narrative. Rather than concentrating on these perceived deficits, which are often heightened by challenging environments, students can redirect their attention toward the attributes that empower them. Here is what you can do in order to achieve this goal:

- Start your day by listing three things you are grateful for regarding your educational journey.

- Reflect on past achievements that highlight your strengths.

- Regularly acknowledge the opportunities that come your way, no matter how small they may seem.

- Maintain a gratitude journal where you note these observations consistently.

By embedding these practices into daily life, one can gradually reframe their perspective, focusing on potential rather than constraint. Over time, this shift can invigorate a mindset ripe for success, fostering resilience and optimism vital during exams.

Affirming positive qualities and past achievements can significantly boost self-esteem and confidence. This isn't about empty flattery; it's about reminding oneself of genuine accomplishments and inherent worth. When stressful situations arise, such as exam settings, negative inner dialogue can commence, undermining one's capabilities just when self-assurance is most needed.

Instead of falling into this pattern, consciously affirming one's positive attributes and previous successes can act as a buffer against doubt and anxiety. Think of times when you've already overcome obstacles or excelled in a subject area. By reaffirming these moments, you reinforce the mental narrative that you are capable and worthy.

For example, consider rehearsing statements like, "I handled that challenging work project effectively," or "I excelled in my last course despite its difficulty." These affirmations anchor self-perception in verifiable facts, counterbalancing the inclination towards self-criticism. The practice here isn't necessarily rigid—it's flexible and akin to muscle memory: the more you flex those "confidence muscles," the sturdier they become, especially under stress.

Reciting positive affirmations regularly can rewire negative thought patterns. Psychological studies substantiate that repeated positive self-statements can reconstruct neural pathways, diverting them away from habitual negativity. This process is akin to retraining the brain to adopt an encouraging internal monologue over a demoralizing one.

To implement this, establish a routine where you articulate affirmations consistently. Choose affirmations that resonate personally, such as "I am equipped to handle this material" or "My efforts today will yield fruitful results."

Here is what you can do to make this a sustained habit:

- Identify your key affirmations based on areas where you need the most encouragement.
- Recite these affirmations aloud each morning and before bedtime.
- Incorporate these affirmations into your study sessions to maintain a positive mental framework.
- Use visual reminders, like sticky notes or digital alerts, to prompt recitation throughout the day.

Through constant repetition, these affirmations gradually fortify your cognitive framework, enhancing mental resilience and paving the way for a more optimistic outlook, particularly during high-pressure scenarios like exams.

Engaging in daily gratitude exercises and affirmations can enhance overall well-being. Positive psychology emphasizes holistic practices that uplift both emotional and physical health. When ingrained into a daily regimen, these practices foster an enduring state of well-being, crucial for academic success.

Daily exercises could be simple yet impactful:

- Write down three things you're grateful for each night before bed.
- Practice mindfulness meditation that centers around themes of gratitude and positivity.
- Share your affirmations with a study group or partner, creating a collective reinforcement system.
- Allocate specific times in your schedule dedicated solely to reflection and affirmation recitals.

These activities don't merely bolster immediate exam performance; they contribute to long-term personal growth and happiness. Cultivating such habits helps create a supportive internal environment where stressors are less likely to escalate into debilitating anxiety. The overall result is an enhanced ability to remain balanced and determined, no matter the external pressures presented by exam scenarios.

By maintaining these practices, students can build a psychological foundation robust enough to withstand the rigors of academic challenges. Consistent practice of gratitude and positive affirmations can indeed foster a resilient and optimistic mindset for approaching exams. Through deliberate engagement with these exercises, you can ensure that you meet exam stress not with trepidation, but with confidence and poise, equipped not just for success in exams but for broader challenges life may present.

Remember, this journey isn't merely about passing exams—it's about equipping yourself with tools for lifelong resilience and well-being. In fostering a consistent gratitude and affirmation practice, you're investing in an internal resource pool that will serve you endlessly, far beyond the confines of academic pursuit. This investment not only enhances your capacity to handle immediate academic obligations but primes you for a future of continuous growth and fulfillment.

Visualizing Success and Past Achievements

Imagining successful exam outcomes can build self-assurance and mental readiness. By creating a vivid mental image of yourself doing well, you signal to your brain that success is achievable. Think about the moments right after you receive your exam results, feeling proud and accomplished. Picture the congratulatory messages from friends and the sense of relief and pride that accompanies seeing your hard work pay off. This technique is backed by research showing that visualizing positive outcomes can positively affect performance and reduce anxiety. When you regularly engage in this practice, it becomes part of your mental routine, making it easier for you to approach exams with confidence and calmness.

Here is what you can do in order to achieve the goal:

- Find a quiet space where you won't be disturbed.
- Close your eyes and take a few deep breaths to relax.
- Imagine yourself sitting in the exam room, feeling focused and calm.
- Visualize opening the exam paper and knowing the answers with clarity.
- Picture completing the exam with time to spare, reviewing your answers confidently.
- Finally, see yourself receiving excellent results and experiencing the joy of achieving your goals.

As you adopt this practice, you'll notice a subtle but significant shift in your mental preparedness for exams. Imagining success places you in a proactive mindset, reducing the likelihood of being overwhelmed by stress or anxiety. It prepares your mind to perform at its best, reinforcing the belief that you are capable of succeeding.

Reflecting on past academic triumphs can serve as a source of inspiration and empowerment. Remember the times when you overcame obstacles and achieved excellent results in your studies. These memories are valuable resources; they remind you of your capabilities and strengths. Look back at those moments when you felt particularly proud of your achievements, and recall the effort and determination that led to your success.

By revisiting these experiences, you create a reservoir of positive reinforcement that you can draw upon whenever you need a confidence boost. This reflection process isn't about dwelling on the past but using it as a stepping stone for future triumphs. Think about how you prepared for those successful exams—what strategies worked, how you managed your time, and the mental attitude you maintained. Allow these reflections to guide you as you prepare for new challenges.

Visualizing overcoming challenges can reduce anxiety and enhance belief in one's abilities. It's not uncommon to encounter difficulties or uncertainties during the preparation for an exam. Instead of allowing these potential setbacks to overwhelm you, try visualizing yourself successfully navigating through them. Imagine a scenario where you face a challenging question on the exam, and then visualize yourself calmly reasoning through it, applying your knowledge, and arriving at the correct answer.

Here is what you can do in order to achieve the goal:

- Identify specific challenges you worry about facing during the exam.
- Envision yourself encountering these challenges without panic.
- See yourself employing effective problem-solving techniques.
- Picture the sense of accomplishment when you overcome the difficulty.
- Practice this visualization regularly to build resilience.

This kind of mental rehearsal helps to desensitize you to the fear of failure. By repeatedly practicing how to handle tough situations in your mind, you're teaching your brain that you have the tools and abilities needed to tackle any challenge. Your brain becomes more adaptable, and the anxiety associated with unpredictability decreases. You start to approach exams with a problem-solving mindset, ready to handle whatever comes your way with confidence and composure.

Creating detailed mental images of success can reinforce positive emotions and motivation. Visualization isn't just about seeing yourself succeed in a general sense but also about including as many sensory details as possible. The more vivid and detailed your mental images, the more real they become to your brain. Imagine the environment around you during the exam—the lighting, the sounds, the feel of the pen in your hand or the keyboard under your fingers.

Focus on the emotions you'd experience—calm, confident, determined—as you go through the exam. Visualize your posture, the way you're sitting upright and alert, the ease with which you navigate through the questions. Picture the look of satisfaction on your face as you complete each section, knowing you've done your best. These mental images serve as powerful motivators, keeping you focused and driven throughout your preparation.

Here is what you can do in order to achieve the goal:

- Spend a few minutes each day practicing this detailed visualization.
- Include all five senses in your mental imagery to make it as realistic as possible.
- Emphasize positive feelings and reframe any negative thoughts.
- Use these visualizations to maintain high motivation levels during study sessions.

When you fill your mind with detailed, positive imagery, you condition yourself to associate exams with success rather than stress. This not only bolsters your motivation but also cultivates a resilient mindset. You're training your brain to expect success, making it more likely that you'll perform well when the actual exam day arrives.

Key takeaways from this discussion include the understanding that the visualization of success and past achievements can instill confidence and drive for academic excellence. By imagining successful outcomes, reflecting on previous academic victories, visualizing overcoming challenges, and creating detailed mental images of success, you can significantly improve your mindset and performance. Employing these techniques consistently can transform your approach to exams, reducing anxiety and boosting your confidence.

Ultimately, the goal is to find a balance between personal responsibility and the necessary support systems that help you thrive. Just like in policy-making where we strive to balance economic growth and human welfare, here we aim to balance solid preparation with mental resilience. When you harness the power of positive psychology and empirical evidence, you're setting yourself up for both immediate success in your exams and long-term personal development.

Cultivating a Growth Mindset

Believing in the potential for growth and improvement can lead to resilience in the face of setbacks. This fundamental principle of positive psychology, known as a "growth mindset," is central to overcoming academic challenges. The idea that abilities and intelligence can be developed through dedication and hard work fosters a resilience that is crucial for facing life's inevitable setbacks. Here's what you can do to cultivate this mindset:

- Acknowledge your current capabilities while believing in the possibility of improvement.
- Regularly seek feedback and use it to identify areas for growth.
- Practice self-compassion by recognizing that effort is a journey towards mastery, not an indicator of inherent ability.

By internalizing these practices, you begin to see setbacks not as failures but as opportunities for growth. This shift in perspective helps mitigate the paralyzing effect of anxiety, particularly during exams, allowing you to approach each challenge with confidence and perseverance.

Viewing challenges as opportunities for learning and development can reduce fear of failure. This change in perspective transforms obstacles into stepping stones rather than roadblocks. Academic exams are often perceived as high-stakes scenarios where the primary objective is to avoid failure at all costs. However, reframing exams as part of a continuous learning process can significantly alleviate pressure.

Imagine you're facing a difficult problem on a test. Instead of fixating on the potential negative outcome, consider how tackling this problem enhances your understanding and skills. This view encourages a more relaxed and open-minded approach to studying and testing. When you see each question as an opportunity to learn rather than a hurdle to clear, the emphasis shifts from performance to personal development. This mindset makes navigating the ups and downs of academic pursuits far less daunting.

Embracing mistakes as part of the learning process can foster perseverance and adaptability. It's essential to understand that mistakes are not definitive judgments of your capabilities. Rather, they are informative markers that can guide your path to improvement. An error made during an exam or in preparation should be seen as a valuable lesson that highlights areas requiring further attention.

Here is what you can do to embrace this principle:

- After encountering errors, take time to reflect on what went wrong and why.
- Develop strategies to address these specific gaps in knowledge or skills.
- Incorporate incremental improvements into your study routine, ensuring consistent progress.
- Surround yourself with supportive peers or mentors who share a similar growth-oriented outlook.

By accepting and learning from mistakes, you build a robust foundation for ongoing growth. This adaptability not only prepares you for future challenges but also instills a sense of resilience that extends beyond academic settings.

Setting goals focused on progress and learning rather than solely on outcomes can enhance motivation. Traditional goal-setting often emphasizes reaching a particular score or grade, which can create undue pressure and anxiety. In contrast, focusing on process-oriented goals—such as mastering a specific concept or improving a particular skill—fosters intrinsic motivation. This type of motivation is rooted in the joy of learning and personal achievement rather than external validation.

For instance, instead of setting a goal to achieve an "A" in a subject, aim to understand the core principles thoroughly and apply them effectively. This subtle shift can make a substantial difference in your approach to studying. Process-oriented goals encourage you to engage more deeply with the material and appreciate the incremental progress made along the way. This focus on continuous development helps maintain enthusiasm and determination, making the learning experience more rewarding and less stressful.

Adopting a growth mindset can shift focus from performance pressure to personal development and continuous improvement. By believing in your potential for growth, viewing challenges as opportunities, embracing mistakes, and setting progress-focused goals, you create an environment where learning thrives. This approach not only reduces anxiety and increases resilience but also makes the educational journey more fulfilling.

In conclusion, cultivating a growth mindset plays a crucial role in transforming the way we perceive and tackle academic challenges. The principles outlined here are grounded in empirical evidence and have shown remarkable efficacy in fostering optimism, resilience, and confidence in various settings. By integrating these concepts into your academic endeavors, you create a proactive strategy that prioritizes human welfare and personal growth over mere performance metrics. This balanced approach not only equips you with the tools needed to excel in exams but also enriches your overall educational experience.

Engaging in Acts of Kindness and Self-Care

Engaging in acts of kindness and self-care to promote well-being and confidence is a powerful strategy, especially for adult students preparing for exams. Let's delve into the multidimensional benefits and practical methods to achieve this goal.

Practicing acts of kindness towards oneself and others can significantly improve mood and self-image. Research has shown that even minor acts of generosity can release endorphins, which elevate our mood, creating a "helper's high." When we extend kindness to others, it reinforces our sense of community and belonging, crucial elements for emotional stability. Start your day with simple gestures such as smiling at someone, holding the door open, or offering a compliment. These seemingly small actions can create ripples of positivity, enhancing your own well-being and confidence.

Here is what you can do in order to achieve the goal:

- Begin with yourself: Treat yourself with the same kindness and understanding as you would a friend. Positive self-talk can transform your internal narrative from doubt to encouragement.

- Make a habit: Develop a routine of performing one kind act daily, whether it's for a family member, colleague, or even a stranger. This consistent practice will gradually foster a more positive self-image.

- Reflect on your actions: Keep a journal to note your acts of kindness and the responses they elicit. This reflective practice can amplify the positive feelings associated with these actions.

Prioritizing self-care activities such as exercise, relaxation, and hobbies is another essential element. Life's demands can often push personal well-being to the backburner. However, investing time in self-care replenishes our mental and physical reserves. Regular exercise, for example, is not just about physical health; it releases neurotransmitters like dopamine and serotonin, which are vital for mood regulation. Find an activity you enjoy—yoga, running, dancing—and make it part of your routine. This can mitigate stress levels and enhance your readiness for exams.

Relaxation techniques such as deep-breathing exercises, progressive muscle relaxation, or even leisurely walks can provide immediate relief from anxiety. Additionally, engaging in hobbies that bring joy, whether painting, gardening, or reading, can be a form of active meditation. These activities engross you fully, providing a much-needed break from academic pressures.

Here is what you can do to incorporate self-care activities:

- Schedule time for exercise: Block out specific times in your calendar for physical activities. Treat these slots with the same importance as your study sessions.

- Practice relaxation techniques: Dedicate a few minutes each day to mindfulness exercises. Apps like Headspace or Calm can guide you through short, effective sessions.
- Pursue hobbies: Allocate time each week to activities purely for enjoyment. Balance is key to maintaining overall well-being, reducing the risk of burnout.

Building a support network of peers and mentors is invaluable. Social connections act as a buffer against stress and provide a platform for emotional reassurance. Engaging with a community of like-minded individuals can foster a sense of shared struggle and collective resilience. Peers going through similar experiences can offer empathy, practical advice, and shared study strategies, while mentors can provide guidance, perspective, and motivation.

Here is how you can establish a robust support network:

- Join study groups: Collaborative learning environments can offer mutual support and aid in addressing academic struggles collectively.
- Seek mentors: Identify instructors or professionals who can serve as mentors. Their experience and insights can help you navigate academic and personal challenges.
- Cultivate relationships: Reach out and nurture relationships with classmates and colleagues. Simple actions like meeting for coffee or forming virtual study circles can strengthen bonds.

Incorporating mindfulness and stress-management techniques into daily routines enhances resilience. Mindfulness practices focus on breathing and present-moment awareness, reducing rumination over past failures or future anxieties. Techniques such as meditation, mindful walking, and body scans encourage a grounded presence, making it easier to manage exam-related stress.

Stress-management strategies like time management, setting realistic goals, and maintaining a balanced lifestyle are crucial. By managing your schedule effectively, you can ensure adequate time for study, rest, and recreation, preventing the buildup of chronic stress.

Here's how you can integrate mindfulness and stress-management techniques:

- Start small: Begin with short, manageable periods of mindfulness practice. Even five minutes of focused breathing can significantly reduce anxiety.
- Establish a routine: Consistency is key. Incorporate mindfulness practices into your daily routine, ideally at the same time each day, to build a sustainable habit.
- Use resources: Numerous apps and online resources offer guided meditations and stress-management courses tailored to various needs.

Acts of kindness, self-care, robust social networks, and mindfulness together contribute to emotional wellness and confidence, fostering a positive foundation for exam success. These practices bolster mental fortitude, making challenges more manageable and opening pathways to more effective learning and retention.

Remember, while preparing for exams is undeniably important, maintaining a healthy, balanced life is paramount. It's this balance that ultimately sustains long-term success and fulfillment, both academically and personally. Engage in acts of kindness, prioritize self-care, lean on your support network, and cultivate mindfulness. Together, these strategies will equip you with the resilience to face exams with confidence and peace of mind.

By adopting these principles, you're not only preparing for exams but also investing in a holistic approach to well-being that extends well beyond any academic setting. Embrace these practices to navigate the rigors of exam preparation and harness their power to enrich your overall quality of life.

Harnessing Positive Psychology for Exam Resilience

In this chapter, we have explored the various principles of positive psychology to enhance optimism, resilience, and confidence in exam settings. The focus has been on cultivating gratitude, practicing positive affirmations, visualizing success, maintaining a growth mindset, and engaging in acts of kindness and self-care.

Firstly, we underscored the importance of expressing gratitude to shift attention from limitations to possibilities. By regularly acknowledging strengths and opportunities, students can reframe their perspective, thus fostering a mindset geared towards success. We also discussed how affirming positive qualities and past achievements can boost self-esteem and counteract negative inner dialogue, especially in stressful scenarios like exams.

Following this, we looked at visualization techniques that encourage students to imagine successful outcomes and reflect on past achievements. These practices help build mental readiness and reduce anxiety by vividly picturing oneself succeeding and overcoming challenges. Such detailed mental images reinforce positive emotions, which are crucial for maintaining motivation and confidence during exam preparations.

We further delved into the growth mindset—believing in the potential for improvement through effort and dedication. Viewing challenges as learning opportunities rather than threats helps mitigate fear of failure and promotes perseverance. Embracing mistakes as part of the learning process fosters adaptability, and setting progress-focused goals enhances intrinsic motivation, creating a more fulfilling educational journey.

Finally, we emphasized the significance of acts of kindness and self-care. Simple gestures of kindness towards oneself and others can improve mood and self-image, while prioritizing self-care activities like exercise, relaxation, and hobbies replenishes mental and physical well-being. Building a support network of peers and mentors provides emotional reassurance and practical advice, bolstering resilience against academic stressors.

It is essential to recognize that these strategies collectively contribute to a strong psychological foundation. This foundation not only helps manage exam-related stress but also supports long-term personal growth and emotional health. When students consistently engage in practices that promote well-being, they build the resilience needed to face academic challenges with confidence and poise.

Therefore, as you integrate these principles into your study routine, focus not only on immediate exam performance but also on nurturing lifelong resilience and well-being. By embedding these positive habits into daily life, you invest in an internal resource pool that extends far beyond academics, equipping you for broader challenges ahead. This balanced approach ensures that you meet exam stress with assurance, ready for continuous growth and fulfillment in all aspects of life.

Chapter 8

Nutrition and Lifestyle Strategiesfor Exam Success

The journey to academic excellence is often depicted as an intellectual endeavor, heavily reliant on rigorous study plans and diligent preparation. However, there's a less obvious yet equally significant component that many learners overlook: the role of nutrition, exercise, and lifestyle choices in achieving exam success. Contrary to common belief, what you consume, how active you are, and how well you manage your daily routine can significantly affect cognitive function and mood regulation.

Many adult students and professionals preparing for exams tend to focus solely on their study schedules, neglecting the broader picture of overall wellness. Poor nutritional choices such as consuming high-sugar snacks or skipping meals can lead to energy crashes and impaired cognitive function. Similarly, a sedentary lifestyle devoid of physical activity may contribute to increased stress levels and reduced mental clarity. Furthermore, irregular sleep patterns can disrupt memory consolidation and impair information processing. For instance, relying on caffeine for late-night studying might provide short-term alertness but leads to long-term fatigue, making it harder to sustain concentration and performance during exams.

This chapter delves into the multifaceted strategies necessary for optimizing cognitive function and improving exam performance through proper nutrition, regular physical exercise, and sound lifestyle choices. You will explore the benefits of brain-healthy foods like blueberries, fatty fish, and nuts, and how these can be seamlessly integrated into your diet. Additionally, the chapter outlines the impact of physical activity on stress reduction and cognitive enhancement, offering practical steps to include exercise in your routine. Finally, it addresses the importance of sleep and relaxation techniques in maintaining mental clarity and reducing anxiety, providing actionable guidelines to foster a holistic approach to exam preparation.

Boosting Cognitive Function with Brain-Healthy Foods

When preparing for exams, many adult students and professionals often focus solely on study schedules and material coverage, neglecting an equally crucial aspect: nutrition. Exam performance is not just a product of mental preparation, but also a reflection of our diet. Certain foods can profoundly impact cognitive function, mood regulation, and overall mental clarity.

Brain-boosting foods like blueberries, fatty fish, and nuts contain essential nutrients that support brain health and cognitive function. For example, blueberries are rich in antioxidants which help protect your brain from oxidative stress. Fatty fish such as salmon is packed with omega-3 fatty acids which are vital for maintaining the structure and function of brain cells. Nuts, especially walnuts, contain high levels of DHA—a type of Omega-3 that's been linked to improved cognitive performance.

While the list of beneficial foods is extensive, incorporating these specific items into your daily meals can have a noticeable effect on your mental capabilities. This doesn't require an overhaul of your diet; small changes can lead to significant improvements.

Here is what you can do to integrate brain-boosting foods into your diet for better cognitive function:

- Start your day with a breakfast smoothie that includes blueberries, spinach, and a splash of flaxseed oil.
- Swap out your usual meat dish at lunch or dinner with a serving of grilled salmon or another fatty fish.
- Replace traditional snacks with a handful of mixed nuts, particularly walnuts and almonds.
- Add leafy greens like kale and spinach into your meals, as they're packed with antioxidants and important vitamins.

Incorporating these foods into your diet can improve focus, memory, and overall mental performance during exams. The mental clarity you gain from such dietary adjustments will be evident in your ability to concentrate for longer periods, retain more information, and articulate answers more precisely under exam conditions. Remember, these benefits are not purely anecdotal but backed by substantial research showing that nutrient-rich foods have a direct correlation with brain function.

To truly benefit from these brain-boosting foods, consistency is key. Make them a regular part of your meals rather than temporary additions leading up to your exams. This ensures that your brain receives a steady supply of essential nutrients.

Consuming a balanced diet rich in antioxidants, omega-3 fatty acids, and vitamins can combat stress and enhance brain function. Antioxidants help reduce oxidative damage, which can impede cognitive function and elevate stress levels. Omega-3 fatty acids play a critical role in neural communication and plasticity—making it easier for your brain to form new pathways and retain information. Vitamins, particularly B vitamins like B6, B12, and folate, are your brain's maintenance crew, helping to keep it in optimal working order.

Guidelines to achieve this:

- Incorporate a variety of colorful fruits and vegetables into each meal to ensure a comprehensive intake of antioxidants.
- Include sources of omega-3s such as chia seeds, flaxseeds, and hemp seeds if you prefer plant-based options over fatty fish.
- Consider a high-quality multivitamin supplement if you struggle to get a wide range of vitamins through food alone.

These dietary strategies serve more than just academic purposes—they improve overall well-being and resilience against stress. Managing exam anxiety is significantly easier when your body isn't coping with the added stress of poor nutrition.

Key takeaways: Prioritize nutrient-dense foods to nourish your brain and optimize cognitive performance during exam periods. It's worth noting that while brain-boosting foods are incredibly important, they should be part of a broader strategy that includes regular physical exercise, adequate sleep, and stress-management techniques.

Physical exercise increases blood flow to the brain, facilitating better oxygen and nutrient delivery, which in turn enhances cognitive function. Aim for activities that get your heart rate up, like brisk walking or cycling, for at least 30 minutes a day. Sleep, on the other hand, allows your brain to consolidate memories and process information, making it indispensable for effective studying and exam readiness. Strive for 7-9 hours of quality sleep each night.

Implementing these lifestyle changes might seem daunting at first, but the payoffs make the effort worthwhile. You'll not only find yourself performing better academically but feeling more energized, less stressed, and healthier overall.

Here are some practical steps to follow:

- Establish a consistent sleep schedule, going to bed and waking up at the same time every day, even on weekends.

- Integrate short bouts of physical activity into your daily routine. If finding a continuous block of time is challenging, try three ten-minute sessions spread throughout the day.

- Manage stress through mindfulness practices such as meditation, deep-breathing exercises, or yoga, which help center your mind and maintain emotional balance.

- Stay hydrated—dehydration can negatively affect your concentration and cognitive abilities. Set reminders to drink water regularly throughout the day.

Remember, optimizing your diet for better brain health does not have to be overly complicated or restrictive. Small, manageable changes made consistently will yield the best results. Balancing these efforts with a holistic approach to wellness creates an environment where your mind can thrive, making exam preparation a less stressful and more successful endeavor.

Adult students and professionals alike will find that taking control of their nutrition can be empowering. Not only will it help mitigate test anxiety and improve exam performance, but it will also foster a greater sense of personal well-being and control over one's life circumstances. Ultimately, the goal is to create a sustainable, evidence-driven approach to nutrition that supports both short-term academic aims and long-term cognitive health.

By focusing on foods that nurture the brain, supplementing with exercise, ensuring ample sleep, and managing stress effectively, you'll unlock your full cognitive potential and approach exams with newfound confidence and clarity.

The Role of Physical Activity in Reducing Stress and Improving Well-being

Regular physical activity, such as aerobic exercises or yoga, can reduce stress hormones and promote a sense of relaxation and mental clarity. The beneficial effects stem from the way exercise influences our body's chemistry. Engaging in activities like brisk walking, swimming, or cycling can lower the levels of cortisol and adrenaline—two stress hormones that contribute to anxiety and tension. Instead, the body begins to produce more endorphins, often called "feel-good" hormones. These changes create a calmer, more focused mental state, which is crucial for anyone preparing for exams.

Incorporating regular exercise into your routine can be straightforward. Here is what you can do in order to achieve the goal:

- Start by choosing an activity you enjoy. The more you like it, the more likely you are to stick with it.

- Aim for at least 30 minutes of moderate-intensity exercise, such as brisk walking or light jogging, most days of the week.

- If finding time is challenging, break your activity into shorter sessions. Even three 10-minute walks spread throughout the day can be beneficial.

- Incorporate flexibility and strength-building exercises once or twice a week. Yoga is particularly effective for combining both physical and mental relaxation.

- Make it a social activity if you can. Exercising with friends or family adds a layer of accountability and enjoyment.

Beyond just reducing stress, exercise also increases blood flow to the brain. When you engage in physical activity, your heart pumps more vigorously, and blood circulation improves. This enhanced blood flow delivers more oxygen and vital nutrients to brain cells, aiding in various cognitive functions like concentration, memory, and problem-solving. Moreover, improved circulation means waste products are efficiently removed from the brain, allowing it to perform optimally. While this might sound technical, the important takeaway is that a well-oxygenated brain is a more efficient brain.

Imagine you're studying for an exam and hitting a mental block. Taking a short break to walk around the block can rejuvenate your brain, making difficult topics seem less daunting when you return. Fresh oxygen and nutrients rush to active brain regions, helping clear out mental fog and enhancing your ability to process information.

Physical movement releases endorphins, neurotransmitters that elevate mood and reduce anxiety, leading to a more positive mindset for exams. Endorphins interact with receptors in your brain, reducing your perception of pain and triggering a feeling of euphoria. This natural high not only makes you feel good but also reduces anxiety levels, creating a more balanced emotional state. For anyone dealing with test anxiety, this shift in mood can be transformative.

Consider those moments when you've felt overwhelmed by the mountain of material you have to study. By including even a short burst of physical activity, you can experience a noticeable improvement in your mood. Whether it's a quick set of jumping jacks, a few minutes of stretching, or even dancing to your favorite song, these activities can quickly lift your spirits and alleviate some of the exam-related tension.

It's essential to recognize that while individual accountability plays a role, having a safety net is equally vital. For instance, institutions can offer spaces that encourage physical activity, such as gyms and outdoor areas. On an individual level, you can plan breaks during long study sessions specifically dedicated to physical movement. Not only does this blend personal responsibility with structural support, but it also sets up a holistic framework where everyone has access to the benefits of exercise.

Exercise should not be viewed as an additional task but as an integrated part of your study routine. Approaching it this way helps in creating a sustainable habit that doesn't feel burdensome. Think of physical activity as a tool in your academic toolkit, one that complements your study techniques, healthy eating habits, and adequate sleep.

In terms of practical steps, start small. Don't overwhelm yourself by attempting to overhaul your entire schedule. Begin with manageable changes and gradually build up your exercise regimen. The cumulative effect over time will be substantial. Consistency is more important than intensity. It's better to engage in moderate physical activity regularly than to have sporadic bursts of strenuous exercise.

Alongside exercise, it's crucial to consider your overall lifestyle choices. Balanced nutrition, sufficient sleep, and stress management strategies all play crucial roles in optimizing cognitive function and exam performance. Each element works synergistically. For example, the benefits of exercise can be amplified when combined with a diet rich in Omega-3 fatty acids, whole grains, and plenty of fruits and vegetables. Proper hydration is equally important, as water helps maintain the optimal functioning of brain cells.

Exam preparation can indeed be stressful, but it doesn't have to be detrimental to your well-being. Recognizing the interconnectedness of physical health, mental clarity, and academic performance allows us to make informed choices that enhance our overall quality of life. Regular physical activity stands out as a simple yet profoundly effective strategy for alleviating stress, boosting mood, and sharpening cognitive abilities, ensuring that we approach exams with confidence and resilience.

The importance of integrating physical activity into daily routines cannot be overstated. It is not just about acing exams but fostering a lifestyle that values and promotes general well-being. By adopting these practices, you're not only setting yourself up for academic success but also investing in long-term health and happiness.

The journey to optimal exam readiness involves more than just hitting the books; it requires a balanced approach that considers both mind and body. By prioritizing regular exercise and making mindful lifestyle choices, you pave the way for a more serene, focused, and effective study experience. As research and evidence continue to show, taking care of your body reaps profound benefits for your mind, ultimately supporting your goals and aspirations.

Prioritizing Sleep for Optimal Cognitive Function

Quality sleep plays a crucial role in memory consolidation, information processing, and overall cognitive performance. Numerous studies show that during sleep, our brains process and consolidate new information, enabling us to recall it more effectively when needed—especially during exams. Furthermore, sleep impacts our ability to understand and connect complex ideas, which is essential for higher-order thinking tasks commonly encountered in academic settings.

Establishing a consistent sleep schedule and creating a relaxing bedtime routine can improve sleep quality and promote mental alertness. This doesn't require drastic lifestyle changes but rather some thoughtful adjustments. Here's what you can do:

- First, aim to go to bed and wake up at the same time each day, even on weekends. Consistency reinforces your body's natural sleep-wake cycle, making it easier to fall asleep and wake up.

- Second, create a pre-sleep ritual that signals to your body it's time to wind down. This could include activities such as reading a book, taking a warm bath, or practicing mindfulness meditation. These routines help transition from wakefulness to sleepiness more smoothly.

- Third, limit exposure to screens at least an hour before bedtime. The blue light from phones, tablets, and computers can interfere with the production of melatonin, a hormone that regulates sleep.

- Fourth, ensure your sleeping environment is conducive to rest. Keep the room cool, dark, and quiet, and consider using earplugs or a white noise machine if you're sensitive to background sounds.

Adequate rest allows the brain to recharge, optimize hormonal balance, and enhance focus and concentration for effective exam preparation. When we are well-rested, our brains are better equipped to handle stress and maintain emotional stability. This is particularly beneficial during intense study periods when managing test anxiety becomes crucial. Studies have shown that sleep deprivation impairs our ability to concentrate, solve problems, make decisions, and control emotions—factors that are all indispensable for peak exam performance.

By prioritizing adequate sleep and rest, you not only bolster your cognitive abilities but also foster a healthier mental state. Remember that sleep is not just passive downtime; it is active recovery time for your brain. So, treat sleep with the same respect and attention as you would any other fundamental aspect of your exam preparation strategy.

Another element to acknowledge is the impact of nutrition on cognitive function. A balanced diet rich in fruits, vegetables, whole grains, and lean proteins provides the necessary nutrients that support brain health. For instance, omega-3 fatty acids found in fish are known to enhance memory and learning. Vitamins like B6, B12, and folic acid contribute to brain development and function, reducing the risk of cognitive decline.

Furthermore, staying hydrated is essential. Even mild dehydration can impair cognitive functions, affecting short-term memory, long-term memory recall, and concentration. Drinking an adequate amount of water daily supports overall brain health and helps maintain mental clarity.

Exercise also plays a critical role in maintaining cognitive function and mood regulation. Regular physical activity increases blood flow to the brain, supplying it with oxygen and essential nutrients. It promotes neuroplasticity—the brain's ability to adapt and reorganize—which enhances learning and memory capabilities. Additionally, exercise triggers the release of endorphins, chemicals that act as natural painkillers and mood elevators, helping to combat stress and anxiety associated with exams.

Combining a nutrient-rich diet with regular exercise creates a synergistic effect on cognitive performance and mood. Physical activities such as walking, jogging, swimming, or even yoga can significantly reduce anxiety levels while improving focus and mental resilience. Integrating these habits into your routine can make a substantial difference in how well you perform academically and manage exam-related stress.

It is equally important to address lifestyle choices that may hinder cognitive function. High levels of stress, excessive consumption of caffeine and alcohol, and irregular sleep patterns can all negatively affect your brain's performance. Stress, in particular, releases cortisol, a hormone that, in high levels, can damage the brain's hippocampus, where memories are formed and stored. Finding healthy ways to manage stress is paramount. Techniques such as deep breathing exercises, progressive muscle relaxation, and guided imagery can be effective tools in reducing stress levels and improving overall mental well-being.

In summary, achieving optimal cognitive function and enhancing exam performance involves a holistic approach where sleep, nutrition, exercise, and lifestyle choices play interconnected roles. Prioritize sufficient sleep duration and quality rest as essential components of exam success and cognitive well-being. Establishing a consistent sleep schedule, focusing on a balanced diet, engaging in regular physical activity, and managing stress constructively are all key strategies. Each element contributes uniquely to brain health and cognitive efficiency, underscoring the importance of integrating these practices into your daily routine.

By adopting these evidence-based strategies, you empower yourself to perform at your best during exams while maintaining a balanced and healthy lifestyle. Remember, true excellence in academics goes beyond cramming and sleepless nights. It requires nurturing your body and mind through deliberate, consistent, and informed choices.

Incorporating Relaxation Techniques for Exam Success

In today's fast-paced and highly demanding academic environment, it's crucial to equip ourselves with effective strategies for managing stress and enhancing performance. One particularly powerful approach involves the integration of relaxation techniques into our daily routines. By focusing on practices such as meditation, deep breathing, and progressive muscle relaxation, we can activate the body's relaxation response, mitigating anxiety and fostering mental clarity.

Meditation is a time-tested method that involves directing attention inward to cultivate a state of calm and heightened awareness. Simple meditation practices, such as sitting quietly and focusing on your breath or repeating a calming mantra, can effectively reduce stress levels. Emphasizing consistency in practice, even for just a few minutes a day, yields substantial benefits over time. The effects are not only immediate but also cumulative, meaning that regular meditation leads to long-term improvements in both mental and emotional well-being.

Deep breathing exercises focus on slow, deliberate breaths to engage the parasympathetic nervous system, responsible for the body's rest-and-digest functions. By taking deep, controlled breaths, we signal our body to relax, lowering heart rate and reducing blood pressure. This simple technique can be employed anywhere, anytime—whether it's before an exam, during a study break, or even while commuting. Consistent practice can help make this calming response more automatic, enabling us to handle stressful situations with greater poise and control.

Progressive muscle relaxation (PMR) is another beneficial practice where one tenses and then slowly releases different muscle groups in the body. This technique helps us become more aware of physical tension and teaches us how to release it consciously. PMR combines well with deep breathing, enhancing the overall relaxing effect. Regular practice of PMR can lead to reduced baseline levels of muscle tension and greater physical comfort, which can positively impact cognitive functions like memory and attention, critical for exam performance.

To integrate these practices into your routine, consider the following:

- Begin by setting aside a dedicated time each day, preferably at the same time, to create a habit.

- Find a quiet space free from distractions to maximize the effectiveness of these practices.

- Start with short sessions, gradually increasing the duration as you become more comfortable with each technique.

- Use guided resources, such as apps or online videos, to help structure your practice, especially if you are new to these techniques.

- Reflect on your experiences and adjustments you may need; personalization ensures that the practices fit comfortably into your routine.

Moving beyond individual techniques, engaging in mindfulness activities and broader relaxation exercises can significantly enhance emotional balance, resilience, and focus, especially during exam periods. Mindfulness emphasizes living in the present moment with full awareness, without judgment. It can be as simple as paying close attention to everyday activities, like eating or walking, with deliberate focus and curiosity.

Incorporating mindfulness into our daily lives doesn't necessarily require additional time set aside specifically for practice. Instead, it's about transforming mundane activities into opportunities for mindfulness. For instance, when studying, focus fully on the material rather than multitasking. Observe your thoughts, feelings, and physical sensations as they arise without trying to change them. Over time, this mindful approach can reduce stress and improve concentration, directly benefiting your study sessions and exam readiness.

Another valuable aspect of managing stress is recognizing the power of daily stress-reducing practices. These routines foster overall well-being, support cognitive function, and cultivate a sense of calm conducive to exam success. When integrated seamlessly into our daily lives, they form a holistic approach to maintaining mental health.

Engaging in physical activities like yoga or tai chi combines movement with mindfulness, offering double the benefit. Both involve slow, deliberate movements synchronized with breath, promoting relaxation and physical flexibility. Participating in these activities regularly not only reduces stress but also improves mood regulation and cognitive functions, important factors in performing well under pressure.

Additionally, incorporating hobbies or creative pursuits can serve as excellent outlets for stress relief. Activities like painting, playing a musical instrument, gardening, or even cooking can provide a mental escape from academic pressures, allowing your mind to reset and recharge. These activities foster a state of flow where time seems to fly by, resulting in rejuvenation and enhanced creativity when you return to your studies.

Here is what you can do to weave these stress-reducing practices into your daily life:

- Develop a balanced schedule that includes regular breaks and leisure activities.

- Prioritize good sleep hygiene; aim for 7-9 hours of restful sleep per night.

- Maintain a healthy diet rich in nutrients that support brain function, such as omega-3 fatty acids, antioxidants, and vitamins.

- Stay hydrated throughout the day to ensure optimal brain performance.

- Create a supportive social network by staying connected with family and friends who provide emotional support during challenging times.

Finally, embracing a positive mindset and practicing gratitude consistently can play a significant role in stress management. Keeping a journal where you note down things you are grateful for each day helps shift focus from what's going wrong to appreciating what's going right. This simple yet powerful practice can elevate mood, increase resilience, and foster an optimistic outlook, all of which are crucial during high-pressure periods like exams.

By integrating these relaxation techniques and stress-reducing practices into your daily routine, you will be better equipped to manage anxiety, improve focus, and maintain a balanced mental state. This comprehensive approach not only prepares you for exam success but also promotes enduring well-being, ensuring you navigate academic challenges with confidence and composure.

Achieving Exam Success Through Balanced Nutrition and Lifestyle Choices

Throughout this chapter, we have delved into the significant impact that nutrition, exercise, and lifestyle choices can have on cognitive function, mood regulation, and exam performance. By exploring brain-healthy foods, the role of physical activity, the necessity of quality sleep, and effective relaxation techniques, we've illuminated how these elements are interconnected in fostering academic success and overall well-being.

As emphasized initially, the journey to optimal exam readiness goes beyond mere cramming and sleepless nights. It involves a balanced approach where diet, physical activity, sleep, and stress management play crucial roles. Our current position underscores the importance of integrating these facets holistically into daily routines. While it might seem overwhelming at first, adopting small, manageable changes can yield profound benefits over time.

What should concern some readers is the potential neglect of one or more aspects discussed, leading to an imbalance. For instance, focusing solely on study material while disregarding nutrition or adequate rest can undermine your efforts and result in diminished performance. Similarly, ignoring physical activity or effective stress-management techniques can leave you vulnerable to anxiety and cognitive fatigue, hindering your exam preparation and overall health.

On a broader scale, the consequences of not adopting these holistic strategies can extend beyond exams. Long-term cognitive decline, chronic stress, and mental health issues are potential risks that highlight the necessity of nurturing both mind and body consistently. Cultivating these habits not only aids in immediate goals like exam performance but also supports lifelong cognitive health and emotional resilience.

As you continue your academic journey, remember the power of small, consistent steps. By prioritizing a nutrient-rich diet, regular physical activity, quality sleep, and effective stress management, you set yourself up for success, not just academically but in all areas of life. Embrace these practices as part of your everyday routine, and discover the remarkable difference they make in achieving your full potential.

Chapter 9

Seeking Support and Resources for Test Anxiety

Test anxiety can be an overwhelming barrier to academic success. One moment, you're brimming with confidence as you review your notes; the next, a simple question leaves your mind blank and your palms sweaty. Many individuals face this challenge, feeling their hard work and preparation unravel under pressure. Recognizing that such anxiety is not merely a fleeting nervousness but a complex issue that can severely impact performance is crucial for finding ways to manage it effectively.

Test anxiety involves more than just last-minute jitters. It encompasses a range of psychological and physical symptoms such as racing thoughts, difficulty concentrating, rapid heartbeat, and even nausea. Imagine preparing for weeks only to feel your confidence evaporate when faced with the exam paper. This experience is all too familiar for many students and can lead to a cycle of chronic stress and diminished self-esteem. Understanding these symptoms and acknowledging their impact helps in taking the first steps towards addressing the problem head-on.

In this chapter, we will explore various avenues for obtaining support and resources to tackle test anxiety. From professional counseling services that provide a safe space to unpack underlying issues, to online tools that offer convenient strategies for anxiety management, the goal is to present practical solutions tailored to different needs. Additionally, we will delve into the benefits of peer support and study groups, highlighting how collaborative efforts can foster resilience and shared strength. By navigating these resources, readers can find effective methods to manage anxiety and enhance their academic performance.

Counseling Services and Therapy

Counseling services provide a safe space to explore underlying issues contributing to test anxiety and develop coping strategies. Many of us tend to underestimate the complexity of test anxiety, often attributing it to mere nervousness or lack of preparation. However, the roots can go much deeper, encompassing a variety of psychological factors such as fear of failure, lack of self-esteem, or past negative experiences with exams. Engaging with counseling services allows you to peel back these layers in a supportive and confidential environment. By doing so, you can start identifying specific triggers and patterns that exacerbate your anxiety. This understanding is the first crucial step towards developing effective coping mechanisms tailored to your individual needs.

Therapy sessions can help individuals challenge negative thought patterns and learn relaxation techniques to reduce anxiety levels. Often, our minds are our own worst enemies; entrenched in cycles of negative thinking that make us believe we aren't capable or worthy. A therapist can help you break down these thought patterns, making it easier to replace them with positive affirmations and constructive thoughts. Additionally, therapy provides an arsenal of relaxation techniques designed to calm the mind and body. These can range from mindfulness exercises, deep-breathing techniques, to progressive muscle relaxation.

Here is what you can do in order to achieve the goal:

- First, identify a licensed mental health professional experienced in treating anxiety disorders. Checking credentials and reviews can guide your choice.

- Second, schedule an initial consultation to discuss your specific concerns and goals for therapy.
- Next, commit to regular sessions to build a rapport with your therapist, which is key to effective treatment.
- Practice the relaxation techniques introduced during therapy in your daily routine. Consistency will enhance their effectiveness.
- Lastly, maintain open communication with your therapist about what works for you and what doesn't, allowing adjustments to be made for optimal benefits.

Collaborating with a trained professional can offer personalized support and guidance tailored to individual needs. Unlike generic advice found in books or online articles, one-on-one sessions with a counselor or therapist are customized just for you. This personalized approach ensures that the interventions and strategies align closely with your unique situation. For instance, if you struggle with time management, a counselor might work with you on procrastination techniques or setting realistic study schedules. If perfectionism is your issue, they might focus on ways to embrace imperfection and adopt a growth mindset. The individualized attention ensures that no stone is left unturned and all facets contributing to your anxiety are addressed comprehensively.

Seeking counseling or therapy is a proactive step towards improving mental well-being and academic performance. It's easy to fall into the trap of believing that seeking help is a sign of weakness, especially when societal norms often glorify self-reliance. However, taking action to address your anxiety through professional means is perhaps one of the most empowering steps you can take. It shows a commitment to your mental health and acknowledges that sometimes we all need a little expert guidance. Proactive engagement in counseling or therapy can also have ripple effects on other aspects of your life, such as improved relationships and better overall emotional stability, enabling you to bring your best self not only to your studies but to all endeavors.

Professional support can empower individuals to address test anxiety holistically and build resilience for future challenges. Dealing with test anxiety isn't just about passing your next exam; it's about long-term mental wellness. Building resilience through professional support means you're equipping yourself with skills that will aid you throughout various life stages and situations. Whether it's future academic pressures, career-related stress, or personal challenges, the strategies and insights gained from counseling and therapy serve as valuable tools that fortify your ability to cope effectively. As you become more adept at managing stress and anxiety, you'll likely find your confidence growing, paving the way for greater academic achievements and personal growth.

In conclusion, navigating the maze of available support systems, resources, and professional help can feel daunting, but it is worth every bit of effort. Counseling and therapy offer structured, empirical-based approaches to tackle test anxiety head-on. By exploring underlying causes, challenging negative thoughts, learning relaxation techniques, and receiving personalized guidance, you can transform how you handle academic pressures. Remember, seeking help isn't a sign of defeat; it's an investment in your well-being and future success. Empowered by professional support, you stand a better chance at not just overcoming test anxiety but thriving in your educational pursuits and beyond.

Online Resources and Self-Help Tools

Online resources provide convenient access to information on anxiety management techniques and self-care practices. In today's digital age, a wealth of knowledge is just a few clicks away. Websites dedicated to mental health, educational blogs, and reputable portals offer evidence-based strategies for managing test anxiety effectively. These online platforms break down complex psychological concepts into digestible content that can be easily understood and implemented in daily life. Whether it's learning about mindfulness practices, breathing exercises, or understanding the biological responses to stress, the convenience of accessing this information online cannot be overstated.

Self-help tools, such as relaxation apps and cognitive-behavioral therapy (CBT) worksheets, offer practical strategies for reducing test anxiety. These tools bring professional-grade methods directly to your fingertips. Relaxation apps often feature guided meditations, progressive muscle relaxation exercises, and ambient soundscapes designed to calm the mind. CBT worksheets, on the other hand, help individuals identify and challenge negative thought patterns, replacing them with positive affirmations and logical reasoning. Here is what you can do to effectively use these tools:

- Begin by exploring various relaxation apps available on app stores; look for ones with high ratings and good reviews.

- Set aside a specific time each day to engage with these apps—consistency makes a significant difference.

- For CBT worksheets, print them out or keep digital copies handy and set a goal to complete one worksheet per week.

- Reflect on your experiences and jot down any improvements or challenges you encounter.

Virtual support communities and forums can provide a sense of belonging and shared experiences for individuals dealing with test anxiety. Participating in these communities allows you to connect with others who face similar struggles. Sharing stories, discussing coping mechanisms, and offering mutual support can be incredibly empowering. The anonymity many forums provide also encourages more open and honest discussions, free from the fear of judgment. It's not uncommon to find solace in knowing that you're not alone and to learn new strategies others have found useful.

Incorporating online resources into daily routines can enhance self-awareness and emotional regulation skills. Simple habits like starting your day with a five-minute meditation or ending it with a reflective journal entry can have profound impacts over time. Monitoring your progress through apps or journaling can increase your awareness of triggers and stressors, helping you to develop better coping mechanisms. Here's how you can start integrating these resources into your lifestyle:

- Select a few key resources that resonate most with you; whether it's an app, website, or online course.

- Dedicate a particular part of your day, such as early mornings or late evenings, to engage with these resources.

- Track your progress by keeping notes or using tracking features available in most apps; this helps to maintain motivation and observe behavioral changes.

- Adjust your routine as needed based on what seems to work best for you over time.

Utilizing online resources can complement professional support and empower individuals to take proactive steps in managing test anxiety. While seeking help from therapists or counselors is invaluable, integrating self-help tools and online resources offers additional layers of support. It equips you with daily practices that reinforce therapeutic goals and provides accessible solutions during stressful moments. By taking ownership of your anxiety management journey, you not only enhance your resilience but also build long-term emotional and mental well-being.

It's easy to see the benefits of fitting these tools and resources into one's daily life. For instance, combining professional therapy sessions with consistent use of CBT worksheets can accelerate the process of developing healthier thought patterns. Likewise, joining virtual support groups while practicing mindfulness using apps can create a balanced approach that addresses both cognitive and emotional aspects of test anxiety.

Another advantage of online resources is their adaptability to individual needs and schedules. Unlike fixed appointments with professionals, online tools and communities can be accessed anytime, providing flexibility for busy adult students and professionals. This flexibility ensures that support is available whenever it's needed, making it easier to stick to anxiety management practices consistently.

Moreover, many online resources are updated regularly to reflect the latest research and trends in mental health management. This means you have access to current, evidence-based practices that can yield effective results. Keeping up with these updates can also instill a sense of ongoing learning and improvement, which is particularly beneficial for those striving to overcome test anxiety.

In conclusion, the strategic use of online resources and self-help tools presents a practical, complementary approach to managing test anxiety. With the right blend of technology and self-discipline, anyone can harness these resources to develop robust coping strategies and achieve a greater sense of control over their anxiety. As you explore and integrate these tools into your life, remember that every small step towards managing test anxiety is a significant stride towards overall mental and emotional wellness. Take advantage of the digital age's offerings and embark on a journey towards a calmer, more confident you.

Peer Support and Study Groups

Navigating available support systems, resources, and professional help for managing and overcoming test anxiety effectively is a multi-faceted endeavor. Engaging in peer support and study groups can be transformative in this journey. Peer support networks offer a sense of community and understanding among individuals experiencing similar struggles with test anxiety. These networks are vital because they create an environment where people can share their experiences without fear of judgment and feel genuinely understood. The mutual empathy cultivates a comforting atmosphere, making it easier to cope with anxiety.

Study groups provide opportunities for collaborative learning, sharing study techniques, and building confidence in exam preparation. They offer a structured setting that helps members focus and maintain consistent study habits. If you're considering joining a study group, here is what you can do to make the most out of it:

- Seek like-minded individuals who have a common goal and a similar level of commitment.
- Establish clear objectives for each session to ensure productive outcomes.
- Share diverse study methods and materials, allowing everyone to benefit from different approaches.
- Rotate roles within the group, such as explaining a topic or facilitating discussions, fostering active participation and deeper understanding.

Peer discussions can offer different perspectives and strategies for managing test anxiety effectively. Often, someone else's insight can shed light on an approach you hadn't considered before. Here are some guidelines to engage in meaningful peer discussions:

- Engage actively in conversations, listening closely and respecting divergent viewpoints.
- Share your experiences openly and honestly, which encourages others to do the same.
- Try new strategies suggested by peers, and provide feedback on their effectiveness.
- Create a supportive environment by celebrating small successes together, reinforcing positive behaviors and attitudes.

Participating in peer support activities can alleviate feelings of isolation and enhance motivation during challenging times. When battling test anxiety, feeling alone in your struggle can exacerbate stress levels. However, knowing that others are facing similar challenges can be incredibly motivating. To immerse yourself in these activities effectively:

- Attend regular meetings or sessions to build continuity and trust within the group.
- Take initiative in organizing group activities or study sessions, which fosters a sense of responsibility and belonging.
- Offer encouragement to peers who might be struggling more than you at times; it reinforces a culture of support.

- Engage in social activities outside the academic context to deepen bonds and reduce overall stress.

In conclusion, peer support and study groups can foster a sense of belonging, friendship, and academic support to navigate test anxiety with shared experiences. Being part of a community that understands your struggles not only reduces feelings of isolation but also provides practical strategies and emotional support. It turns the daunting process of exam preparation into a collective effort, infusing it with camaraderie and shared success stories.

The intricate balance between individual freedom and social responsibility that we value so much can be mirrored in these peer engagements. You maintain personal control over your studies and strategies while contributing to a larger community working towards the same goal—successfully managing and overcoming test anxiety. The data strongly supports the efficacy of peer-supported learning environments in reducing anxiety and improving academic performance, so it becomes imperative that we embrace these communal frameworks.

Let's remember, while navigating our educational journeys, that cooperation and mutual aid often lead to better outcomes than solo endeavors. So, as you step forward into the labyrinth of exams and anxieties, consider reaching out to those around you. Form or join a peer support network or study group. It's a tangible, evidence-backed way to transform test anxiety from a solitary struggle into a shared challenge, faced hand-in-hand with fellow travelers on the path to success.

Academic Accommodations

Navigating the labyrinth of academic accommodations may initially seem daunting, but it is a powerful step toward managing test anxiety and promoting equal opportunities for all students. One of the most effective methods to alleviate stress levels is through specific accommodations such as extended time or a quiet testing environment. These modifications can significantly reduce pressure during exams, providing a more supportive setting that allows students to demonstrate their true capabilities.

Here is what you can do to secure these accommodations:

- Begin by reaching out to your institution's disability support services. This department is typically well-versed in the process of arranging accommodations.

- Obtain documentation from a licensed mental health professional or medical provider. This documentation should detail your diagnosis of test anxiety and explain how it impacts your ability to perform under standard testing conditions.

- Submit this documentation along with any required forms to your institution's support services. Ensure that you follow up regularly to track the status of your request.

- Once approved, communicate with your professors to confirm that they are aware of your accommodations well before any scheduled exams. This step helps ensure seamless implementation when test day arrives.

The cooperation between educational institutions and students is vital to standardizing fair opportunities for those affected by test anxiety. By working together, institutions can implement necessary accommodations effectively. This collaborative effort not only benefits individual students but also promotes an inclusive academic environment overall.

To transition smoothly into this collaborative approach, consider the following steps:

- Proactively engage with your professors and educational support services. Open communication about your needs can lead to creative and tailored solutions.

- Attend meetings organized by your educational institution that discuss student accommodations, if available. Your participation underscores the importance of accommodating diverse learning needs.

- Advocate for policy changes at the institutional level, if necessary. This advocacy can help establish or improve existing frameworks for student support.

By maintaining open lines of communication, students and educators alike can foster a more inclusive and understanding learning environment. Sharing your experiences with test anxiety candidly can dismantle potential misconceptions and pave the way for more personalized support strategies.

For instance, speaking openly with your professors about your struggles can yield several benefits:

- Professors may offer alternative assessment methods that align better with your strengths.

- You might receive additional resources or study aids designed to target anxiety management.

- Such dialogues can nurture a sense of empathy and understanding within the classroom, benefiting both you and your peers who might be experiencing similar issues.

Taking proactive steps to seek accommodations illustrates a commitment to overcoming barriers posed by test anxiety. It reflects a recognition of personal limitations and a willingness to address them head-on. This proactive attitude not only helps in optimizing exam performance but also sets a positive example for others who may be reluctant to pursue similar measures due to stigma or uncertainty.

Embracing academic accommodations is essential in leveling the playing field, ensuring that all students have the opportunity to excel based on their knowledge and skills rather than being hindered by anxiety. Furthermore, it supports the broader objective of creating a nurturing and equitable academic environment where every individual can thrive.

Understanding the intricacies involved in securing accommodations is crucial. Each step, from initial contact with support services to ongoing communication with faculty, plays a fundamental role in ensuring successful implementation. The emphasis should always remain on collaboration and mutual understanding, recognizing that the ultimate goal is to create a supportive and inclusive educational experience for everyone.

As adults preparing for academic exams or professionals pursuing further education or certifications, it is imperative to actively seek out and utilize available resources. Confronting test anxiety head-on with strategic and evidence-driven actions will undoubtedly pave the way for academic success and personal growth. By leveraging the support systems in place, you can transform the challenge of test anxiety into an opportunity for empowerment and achievement.

The journey toward managing test-related anxiety may require persistence and patience. However, with the right tools and mindset, it is entirely possible to mitigate its effects and achieve your academic goals. Remember that seeking help is not a sign of weakness but a demonstration of resilience and determination. With each step taken, you are contributing to a more inclusive and supportive academic landscape for yourself and others.

Building Resilience and Empowerment

Navigating available support systems, resources, and professional help for managing and overcoming test anxiety effectively is a multi-faceted endeavor. In this chapter, we have explored counseling services, therapy, online resources, self-help tools, peer support, study groups, and academic accommodations as vital components in managing test anxiety.

Reaching out to counseling services and engaging in therapy can significantly aid in identifying underlying issues and developing coping mechanisms. Therapy provides a structured approach to challenge negative thought patterns and introduces relaxation techniques that are essential for reducing anxiety levels. Identifying and committing to regular sessions with a licensed mental health professional ensures tailored strategies to your specific needs, fostering a supportive environment for personal growth.

On the digital front, online resources and self-help tools offer practical strategies accessible at any time. They equip you with knowledge and techniques such as mindfulness practices and cognitive-behavioral therapy (CBT) exercises. Consistent engagement with these tools enhances self-awareness and emotional regulation, complementing professional support and empowering you to take proactive steps in managing anxiety.

Peer support and study groups are instrumental in creating a sense of community and shared understanding. They provide opportunities for collaborative learning, which can boost confidence and alleviate feelings of isolation. Regular participation and active engagement in these groups foster a supportive network that shares strategies and successes, making the journey less daunting.

Academic accommodations, though sometimes complex to navigate, are crucial in providing equal opportunities for students. Securing accommodations like extended time or a quieter testing environment helps mitigate pressure during exams. Open communication with educational institutions and professors ensures these accommodations are implemented effectively, promoting an inclusive academic setting.

While test anxiety can be overwhelming, the combination of these resources and supports offers a comprehensive approach to tackling it. The consequences of not addressing test anxiety extend beyond academic performance; they impact overall well-being and future resilience. Therefore, taking advantage of these support systems is not just about passing exams but about building long-term mental wellness and resilience.

As you continue on your educational journey, remember that seeking help and utilizing available resources is a demonstration of strength and a commitment to your success. Embracing both professional assistance and self-help strategies allows you to navigate test anxiety more effectively, paving the way for greater achievements and personal development. Through consistent effort and the right support, you can transform test anxiety from a barrier into a manageable aspect of your academic and professional growth.

Chapter 10

Thriving Beyond Test Anxiety: Sustaining Academic Success

For many students and professionals, the period leading up to exams can feel like navigating through a storm. The pressure to perform well, the sheer volume of material to master, and the relentless march of deadlines can collectively create an environment ripe for stress and anxiety. However, what if instead of merely surviving these high-stress moments, one could thrive? Imagine developing a set of skills that not only help manage immediate test-related anxieties but also contribute to sustained academic success and emotional well-being in the long term.

Test anxiety is a common issue that manifests in various ways, from difficulty concentrating and physical symptoms like sweating or a racing heart to disruptive worry and self-doubt. These reactions can hinder performance and derail even the most prepared individuals. Picture a student who has diligently studied for weeks but finds their mind blank the moment they sit for the exam, or a professional whose hands shake during credentialing tests despite hours of preparation. Such scenarios highlight how crippling test anxiety can be, making it clear that effective strategies for managing this stress are essential.

This chapter delves into a comprehensive approach to overcoming test anxiety by integrating sustainable stress management techniques into daily routines. We will explore how practices like mindfulness, regular physical exercise, structured breaks, and deep breathing exercises can significantly enhance both emotional resilience and cognitive function. Each technique offers unique benefits that, when combined, form a robust framework for maintaining calm and focus not just during exams but throughout the academic journey. Join us as we uncover actionable strategies that pave the way for both academic excellence and personal well-being.

Incorporating Stress Management Techniques in Daily Life

Implementing a daily mindfulness practice can be transformative for managing stress and enhancing focus on academic goals. Mindfulness, simply put, is the practice of being fully present in the moment without judgment. For students and professionals grappling with test anxiety, integrating mindfulness into one's daily routine can serve as a powerful tool. Here's what you can do to get started:

- Begin with setting aside just five minutes each day for mindfulness meditation. Find a quiet space where you won't be disturbed, sit comfortably, and close your eyes.

- Focus on your breath, noticing the inhale and exhale. If your mind starts to wander—which it naturally will—gently bring your attention back to your breath without self-criticism.

- As this practice becomes more comfortable, gradually increase the duration to ten or fifteen minutes.

- Some individuals find using guided meditations, available through apps or online resources, helpful for maintaining focus.

Mindfulness not only helps reduce overall stress levels but also enhances cognitive functions such as concentration and memory, which are crucial for academic success. By consistently practicing mindfulness, you equip yourself with a mental toolkit that can be called upon during high-stress moments, like exam preparations or actual test scenarios.

Engaging in regular physical exercise is another cornerstone in managing stress and promoting overall well-being. Physical activity releases endorphins, which are chemicals in the brain that act as natural painkillers and mood elevators. Incorporating exercise doesn't mean you need to become a marathon runner or a gym enthusiast. It's about finding what fits naturally into your lifestyle and interests. Here's how you might integrate regular physical activity:

- Start by identifying a form of exercise that you enjoy. It could be as simple as brisk walking, cycling, swimming, or even dancing.

- Aim for at least 30 minutes of moderate exercise most days of the week. This can be broken down into shorter periods if that suits your schedule better.

- Consider making exercise a social activity by involving friends or joining group classes. This adds an element of accountability and fun.

- Use technological aids like fitness trackers or mobile apps to monitor your progress and set achievable goals.

Regular physical activity not only helps in stress reduction but also improves sleep quality, boosts self-esteem, and enhances cognitive function. This holistic approach ensures that you remain balanced and energized, ready to tackle your academic challenges head-on.

Next, scheduling regular breaks during study sessions is essential to prevent burnout and maintain a healthy work-life balance. Continuous studying without intervals can lead to diminishing returns, where productivity decreases despite the number of hours spent. Here's a strategy to ensure you incorporate effective breaks:

- Adopt the Pomodoro Technique: Work for 25 minutes, then take a five-minute break. After four such cycles, take a longer break of 15-30 minutes.

- During these breaks, step away from your study area. Engage in activities that refresh your mind, such as stretching, taking a short walk, or listening to music.

- Avoid engaging with screens during breaks. This includes refraining from checking social media or watching videos, as screen time does not provide the same relaxation benefits.

- Use your breaks as an opportunity to hydrate and fuel your body with healthy snacks, which can help maintain both physical and mental energy levels.

By conscientiously scheduling these breaks, you allow your brain to process information effectively and return to your studies with renewed focus and motivation. This method promotes not only sustained academic performance but also a healthier and more enjoyable learning experience.

Lastly, practicing deep breathing exercises is an immediate and effective way to calm the mind and improve cognitive function, especially during periods of high stress. Deep breathing activates the body's relaxation response, counteracting the stress response triggered during high-pressure situations like exams. Here's a simple approach to incorporating deep breathing exercises:

- Find a comfortable sitting position and close your eyes to minimize distractions.

- Inhale deeply through your nose, allowing your abdomen to expand as you fill your lungs with air. Count to four as you inhale.

- Hold your breath for a count of four, allowing the oxygen to circulate throughout your body.

- Exhale slowly and completely through your mouth, counting to six as you release the breath.

- Repeat this process several times, focusing on the sensation of the breath moving in and out of your body.

Incorporating deep breathing exercises into your routine doesn't require much time but yields significant benefits. Practicing these exercises regularly trains your body to manage stress more efficiently, providing a calming effect that can be particularly valuable before or during exams.

Key takeaways for maintaining emotional well-being, academic achievement, and resilience beyond exam periods revolve around consistent implementation of these stress management techniques. Establishing a daily mindfulness practice, engaging in regular physical exercise, scheduling breaks, and practicing deep breathing exercises each contribute to building a robust framework for managing stress. By adopting these strategies, you create a sustainable path toward improved emotional resilience and academic performance over time.

Through mindful integration of these practices into your daily life, the journey toward emotional well-being and academic success becomes less daunting and more manageable. Remember, the goal is not perfection but progress. Each small step taken towards managing stress and enhancing focus can accumulate into significant long-term benefits. So, take these strategies to heart, implement them consistently, and you'll likely find yourself not only excelling academically but also thriving personally.

Setting Realistic Academic and Career Goals

When it comes to long-term strategies for maintaining emotional well-being, academic achievement, and resilience beyond exam periods, setting realistic academic and career goals is paramount. This approach not only fosters personal growth but also reduces anxiety and pressure, making the journey more manageable and fulfilling.

First, consider breaking down your long-term academic goals into smaller, more manageable tasks. This can significantly reduce the feelings of being overwhelmed by the enormity of the objective ahead. Here's what you can do to make this process smoother:

- Start by identifying your ultimate goal.

- Divide this goal into intermediate milestones that are achievable within a shorter time frame.

- Break these milestones further down into daily or weekly tasks that you can tick off regularly.

For example, if your long-term goal is to attain a master's degree, focus initially on completing each semester successfully. Within each semester, aim to excel in individual courses by allocating specific tasks such as reading assigned chapters, completing assignments, and engaging in study groups. By taking one step at a time, you create a sense of progress and accomplishment, which is crucial for sustained motivation.

While moving through your academic journey, seeking mentorship or guidance can be immensely beneficial. Mentors provide invaluable insights into potential career paths and academic opportunities that align with your interests and strengths. They help you navigate challenges, offering advice drawn from their own experiences. Seek mentors within your institution, professional networks, or even in online forums related to your field of interest. Establishing these connections can lead to new opportunities and encourage you to pursue goals that resonate deeply with your passions and abilities.

In addition, it's important to embrace failures and setbacks as learning experiences instead of viewing them merely as obstacles. Failure is an inevitable part of any growth process, and it's essential to understand that each setback offers a chance to learn and improve. When faced with a failure, take a step back to analyze what went wrong and identify areas that need improvement. Use this understanding to adjust your strategies and approaches accordingly. Remember, some of the most successful people have faced numerous failures before achieving their goals. It's how they responded to those setbacks that defined their ultimate success.

To maintain a clear direction and ensure your goals remain relevant, regularly reassess and adjust your academic and career aspirations. Here's a practical way to keep your goals aligned with your evolving aspirations:

- Periodically reflect on your progress and experiences.
- Evaluate whether your current goals still excite and motivate you.
- Make adjustments based on new information, interests, or changing circumstances.

By doing so, you stay flexible and prepared to pivot when necessary, ensuring your academic and career goals continue to reflect your true ambitions and potential.

The key takeaways from developing these strategies are profound. Setting realistic goals and fostering a growth mindset not only help sustain motivation but also reduce anxiety, making the pursuit of academic success much more manageable. Embrace the journey with its ups and downs, knowing that each step forward or backward contributes to your holistic development.

There's an undeniable synergy between personal responsibility and the necessity of a supportive safety net. While it's crucial to take charge of your own progress and well-being, acknowledge that seeking support during hard times is equally important. Establish a reliable network of friends, family, and mental health professionals who can provide assistance and encouragement when needed. Emotional well-being is often fortified by having a strong support system, allowing you to navigate both triumphs and trials with greater resilience.

Moreover, it's beneficial to cultivate habits that promote overall well-being alongside academic pursuits. Regular exercise, adequate sleep, a nutritious diet, and mindfulness practices are not just cliches; they are foundational elements that support mental clarity and physical stamina. Creating a balanced routine that includes time for self-care ensures you're not running on empty while striving to meet your goals.

Continuously seeking knowledge outside of formal education also enriches your academic journey. Engage with books, podcasts, seminars, and workshops that pique your curiosity and expand your understanding of various subjects. This not only broadens your perspective but also makes learning more enjoyable and less confined to the pressures of exams and grades.

In conclusion, developing a long-term strategy for maintaining emotional well-being, academic achievement, and resilience hinges on setting realistic goals that evolve with your aspirations. By breaking down larger objectives into manageable tasks, seeking mentorship, embracing setbacks as growth opportunities, and regularly reassessing your goals, you build a robust framework for sustained success. Combine this with a holistic approach to well-being, and you're equipped to handle the rigors of academia and beyond with grace and determination.

It's worth reiterating that the journey towards academic and career accomplishments should never come at the expense of your well-being. Balancing ambition with compassion for yourself creates a sustainable path to success, where you can thrive academically while nurturing your emotional health. In doing so, you establish a resilient foundation that supports not just short-term achievements but a lifelong pursuit of learning and growth. Remember, it's as much about the journey as it is about the destination—nurture both with equal care and intention.

Promoting Self-Compassion and Self-Care Routines

To start, let's address practicing self-compassion by acknowledging and accepting personal limitations and imperfections without self-judgment. Understanding our own limits is crucial for emotional well-being and resilience, especially during high-stress periods like exams. When we constantly criticize ourselves for not meeting certain standards or making mistakes, we diminish our capacity to cope effectively. Instead, recognize that imperfections are an integral part of being human. Everyone encounters moments where they don't quite measure up to their own expectations. The key is to acknowledge these moments compassionately rather than condemning oneself.

Here is what you can do in order to achieve the goal:

- **Pause and Reflect:** When you feel negative self-talk creeping in, take a moment to pause and reflect. What would you say to a friend who is struggling? Extend that same kindness to yourself.
- **Affirmations:** Develop a set of positive affirmations that resonate with you. These can be reminders that you're doing your best under the circumstances.
- **Mindfulness Practices:** Engage in mindfulness exercises to stay grounded in the present moment. Mindfulness can help you observe your thoughts and feelings without judgment.

A well-rounded self-care routine is another cornerstone of maintaining emotional well-being and academic resilience. This includes activities that nurture your emotional, physical, and mental health. Adequate sleep, healthy eating, and relaxation practices such as meditation, yoga, or even simple breathing exercises can significantly enhance your ability to cope with stress. Your body and mind are interconnected; when one suffers, the other is often affected. Therefore, prioritizing a balanced diet and sufficient rest isn't just about physical health but also about optimizing cognitive functions and emotional stability.

Here is what you can do in order to achieve the goal:

- **Adequate Sleep:** Aim for 7-9 hours of sleep per night. Consistency is key—try to maintain a regular sleep schedule even on weekends.
- **Healthy Eating:** Incorporate a variety of fruits, vegetables, whole grains, and lean proteins into your diet. Avoid excessive caffeine and sugar as they can lead to energy crashes and mood swings.
- **Relaxation Practices:** Find what works for you, whether it's deep-breathing exercises, progressive muscle relaxation, or guided imagery. Allocate at least 10 minutes daily to these activities to decompress and recharge.

Setting boundaries is essential for prioritizing personal well-being. In today's hyper-connected world, where the lines between work, study, and leisure often blur, it's vital to carve out time for activities that nourish your soul. Hobbies, social interactions, and leisure activities are not mere indulgences—they are necessities for a balanced life. Engaging in these activities allows you to step away from academic pressures and reminds you that there is more to life than exams and grades.

Here is what you can do in order to achieve the goal:

- **Prioritize Leisure:** Schedule time for hobbies and interests as you would any other important appointment. This could be anything from reading a novel, painting, gardening, or playing a musical instrument.
- **Set Boundaries:** Learn to say no when additional responsibilities threaten your well-being. Communicate clearly with others about your needs and limits.
- **Social Interactions:** Make time for friends and family. Social support is a powerful buffer against stress. Whether it's a quick chat over coffee or a weekend adventure, these interactions provide emotional sustenance.

Lastly, cultivating a positive self-image by focusing on strengths and achievements, rather than dwelling on perceived shortcomings, can dramatically improve both emotional well-being and academic performance. Often, the pressure to excel academically can magnify minor failures, leading to a skewed perception of self-worth. By consciously redirecting focus toward your accomplishments and innate strengths, you create a mental environment conducive to growth and resilience.

Here is what you can do in order to achieve the goal:

- **Strengths Journal:** Keep a journal where you regularly jot down your achievements, big or small. Reflect on the skills and qualities that enabled those successes.

- **Positive Visualization:** Spend a few minutes each day visualizing your past successes and feeling the emotions associated with those moments. This practice can boost your confidence and motivation.

- **Mentorship:** Seek out mentors or role models who can offer guidance and reinforcement of your strengths. Constructive feedback from someone you respect can be incredibly affirming.

Each of these strategies can individually bolster your emotional resilience and academic achievement, but they are most effective when integrated into a holistic approach to self-care and well-being. By prioritizing self-compassion, establishing robust self-care routines, setting clear boundaries, and fostering a positive self-image, you create a foundation from which you can navigate the stresses of exam periods and beyond with greater ease.

It is important to remember that these practices are not just stop-gap measures for crisis times but long-term strategies for building a resilient and balanced life. Emotional well-being and academic performance are not mutually exclusive; they are deeply intertwined, and nurturing one invariably supports the other. Use these guidelines to craft a personalized plan that suits your individual needs and lifestyle, knowing that the investment in yourself will pay dividends far beyond exam success.

Emphasizing Continuous Education and Personal Growth

Engaging in lifelong learning opportunities is a cornerstone of maintaining emotional well-being, academic achievement, and resilience beyond exam periods. The pursuit of knowledge should not end once formal education does; rather, it should be seen as an ongoing journey that enriches our lives and keeps us mentally agile. To achieve this, individuals can explore various avenues such as workshops, seminars, and online courses. These platforms allow for the continuous enhancement of skills and the acquisition of new information that can be directly applicable to one's personal and professional life.

Here is what you can do in order to embrace lifelong learning:

- Seek out workshops or seminars relevant to your field or interests. They provide hands-on experience and offer practical insights that textbooks may not cover.

- Enroll in online courses from reputable institutions. Many universities offer free courses in diverse subject areas that can broaden your horizons.

- Take advantage of webinars and podcasts. These are convenient forms of learning that can be integrated seamlessly into your daily routine.

By incorporating these activities into your routine, you create a fertile ground for intellectual growth and professional advancement.

Pursuing personal growth through experiences that challenge your comfort zone is another crucial aspect. When we step outside our familiar surroundings and engage in activities that stretch our abilities, we develop resilience and foster creativity. This might involve taking up a new hobby, engaging in public speaking, or even traveling to new places. Each of these experiences provides opportunities to learn more about ourselves and the world around us.

To fuel innovation and creativity:

- Try something you've never done before. It could be as simple as trying a new sport or as challenging as learning a musical instrument.

- Engage in creative endeavors like painting, writing, or dancing. These activities not only serve as stress relievers but also spark innovative thinking.

- Volunteer for causes you are passionate about. Volunteering offers new perspectives and teaches problem-solving skills in real-world scenarios.

By regularly stepping out of your comfort zone, you build a robust framework for personal growth that enables you to face challenges with confidence and ingenuity.

Seeking mentorship or networking opportunities is fundamental for both professional and personal development. Having mentors to guide you provides invaluable insights and advice, often stemming from their own experiences. Likewise, networking with peers and professionals in your field can open doors to new opportunities, collaborations, and support systems that are essential for sustained success.

To effectively seek mentorship and network:

- Attend industry conferences and networking events. These gatherings are ideal for meeting like-minded individuals and establishing meaningful connections.

- Join professional organizations or online forums related to your field. They offer platforms to share knowledge and gain advice.

- Don't hesitate to reach out to potential mentors. A simple email expressing your interest in learning from them can initiate a beneficial relationship.

While seeking guidance, remember that networking is a two-way street. Offer your help and expertise whenever possible, fostering a mutually supportive environment.

Reflecting on past achievements and areas for improvement plays a pivotal role in setting new goals that align with long-term growth and fulfillment. Reflection allows for a thoughtful evaluation of what has worked well and where there is room for growth. This introspection is crucial for setting realistic and aspirational goals that keep you motivated.

Here is what you can do to reflect effectively:

- Keep a journal where you document your successes and challenges. Writing about your experiences helps clarify your thoughts.

- Regularly review your past goals and assess your progress. This practice helps in understanding your growth trajectory and identifying patterns.

- Use feedback from mentors, peers, and self-assessment tools. Constructive criticism is invaluable for personal and professional development.

With these reflections, you can set new, informed goals that propel you toward continual improvement.

By embracing continuous learning and personal development, individuals sustain academic success and cultivate resilience, leading fulfilling lives beyond the pressures of exam periods. Balancing economic growth and human welfare means recognizing the value of personal well-being alongside professional accomplishments. Engaging in lifelong learning ensures that your skills remain relevant and your mind sharp, while stepping out of your comfort zone fosters innovation and creative problem-solving. Seeking mentorship and networking builds a reliable support system, and reflective practices ensure that your growth is consistent and aligned with your aspirations.

In summary, the journey to maintain emotional well-being, academic achievement, and resilience extends far beyond exam periods. With a focus on continued education, personal growth, strong networks, and reflective goal-setting, you can build a fulfilling and balanced life. Embrace the evidence-driven approach of integrating empirical data into your strategies, ensuring that each step you take is informed and purposeful. By doing so, you not only enhance your professional and personal life but also contribute positively to the broader societal fabric, embodying the principles of individual freedom and social responsibility.

Maintaining Long-Term Emotional Well-being and Academic Resilience

In this chapter, we have explored strategies aimed at maintaining emotional well-being, academic achievement, and resilience beyond exam periods. From incorporating stress management techniques into daily routines to setting realistic academic goals, each approach contributes to a sustainable and balanced path toward success.

Starting with stress management, practices like mindfulness, regular physical exercise, and deep breathing exercises provide immediate and long-term benefits in reducing stress and enhancing cognitive functions. These techniques empower you with tools to manage anxiety and maintain focus during high-pressure situations, such as exams.

Setting realistic academic and career goals further supports your overall journey by breaking down large objectives into manageable tasks. This method reduces feelings of being overwhelmed and fosters personal growth. The importance of mentorship and embracing failures as learning experiences also cannot be overstated. They offer guidance and valuable insights that help navigate academic challenges effectively.

Self-compassion and self-care routines form another critical pillar in sustaining emotional well-being. By acknowledging personal limitations without self-judgment and prioritizing activities that nourish your mind and body, you build resilience against stressors. Establishing boundaries and engaging in hobbies or leisure activities ensures a balanced lifestyle, preventing burnout.

Continuous education and personal growth extend beyond formal learning environments. Engaging in lifelong learning through workshops, online courses, and new experiences keeps your mind agile and adaptable. Seeking out mentors and networking helps build a support system essential for ongoing development and success. Reflecting on past achievements and areas for improvement ensures that your goals remain aligned with your evolving aspirations.

For some readers, the concern may lie in the feasibility of integrating these varied strategies into their already packed schedules. It is important to remember that small, consistent efforts can lead to significant changes over time. The key is to start with one or two practices that resonate with your current needs and gradually expand to include others.

The consequences of not adopting these strategies could mean continued struggles with stress and anxiety, potentially impeding academic performance and personal growth. On the wider scale, embracing these techniques collectively contributes to a culture where well-being and success go hand in hand, promoting healthier learning environments.

As you move forward, consider these strategies as part of a holistic approach to your academic and personal life. Remember, progress is more important than perfection. Each step you take toward managing stress and enhancing your focus contributes to your long-term well-being and success. Keep an open mind, stay flexible, and allow yourself the grace to grow and adapt along your journey.

Conclusion

Test anxiety is a common issue that plagues many students, often transforming the anticipation of an exam into a source of dread. It can manifest in various ways, from racing thoughts and sweaty palms to a paralyzing fear that disrupts focus and recall. Despite having studied diligently, the overwhelming pressure can impede performance, leading to frustration and discouragement. Understanding this multifaceted problem is the first step towards effectively managing and reducing its impact.

The crux of test anxiety lies in both psychological and physical responses. On a psychological level, negative thought patterns often exacerbate stress. For instance, a student might think, "I always mess up on tests" or "If I fail this exam, my future is ruined." Such thoughts not only drain mental energy but also heighten anxiety levels. On the physical side, symptoms like increased heart rate, shallow breathing, and muscle tension further amplify the feeling of being overwhelmed. These interconnected factors create a vicious cycle that makes exams more daunting than they need to be.

In this chapter, we will delve into a variety of evidence-based strategies designed to manage and reduce test anxiety effectively. You will learn about cognitive-behavioral techniques to reframe negative thinking, breathing exercises to calm the nervous system, and mindfulness practices to cultivate present-moment awareness. Additionally, we will explore how preparation through tailored study plans and emotional regulation can build resilience and improve overall performance. By integrating these approaches, you can transform your exam experience from one of anxiety to one of confidence and clarity.

Summary of Key Points

In managing and reducing test anxiety, evidence-based strategies play an essential role. One of the most effective methods is employing psychological techniques. These can range from cognitive-behavioral approaches to positive thinking exercises. Cognitive-behavioral therapy (CBT), for instance, helps reframe negative thought patterns into more constructive ones. This transformation is particularly helpful when faced with high-pressure situations like exams. Positive affirmations also have their utility; they reinforce a student's belief in their capability and readiness. Consistently reminding oneself of past successes and strengths can build confidence over time.

Breathing exercises are another valuable tool. They serve as immediate remedies for acute stress moments. Techniques such as diaphragmatic breathing or the 4-7-8 method can quickly calm the nervous system. Diaphragmatic breathing involves taking deep breaths that engage the diaphragm rather than shallow chest breaths. The 4-7-8 method involves inhaling for four seconds, holding the breath for seven seconds, and exhaling slowly for eight seconds. These practices help lower heart rates and create a sense of physiological calmness, aiding in stress management during exam preparation and execution.

Mindfulness practices offer a profound way to tackle test anxiety by fostering present-moment awareness. Mindfulness meditation helps in focusing attention on the moment rather than getting entangled in future worries or past regrets. It cultivates an attitude of acceptance and non-judgment towards one's thoughts and feelings, thus reducing anxiety. Practicing mindfulness can be as simple as setting aside a few minutes each day to sit quietly and observe your breath or surroundings. Over time, this practice enhances emotional regulation, allowing students to approach exams with a clearer mind.

Preparation is undeniably vital in mitigating test anxiety. A well-planned study schedule can go a long way in reducing last-minute panic. Breaking down the syllabus into manageable chunks allows for consistent progress and better retention of information. Regular review sessions and self-assessment through mock tests can also reinforce learning and build familiarity with exam formats.

Here is what you can do in order to achieve the goal:

- Create a detailed study plan that specifies daily and weekly goals.
- Break study material into smaller segments for easier assimilation.
- Incorporate regular review sessions to reinforce learning.
- Utilize mock tests and practice exams to gauge your progress.

Emotional regulation is equally crucial in managing test anxiety. Techniques such as journaling and expressive writing can provide an outlet for anxious thoughts and feelings. Keeping a journal where you can freely express your worries about upcoming exams can be incredibly therapeutic. It not only provides relief but also offers insights into recurring thought patterns that may be contributing to anxiety. Identifying and addressing these patterns can reduce their influence over time.

Building psychological resilience is another integral aspect. Resilience equips students to cope with setbacks and persist despite challenges. Strategies for building resilience include developing a growth mindset, where challenges are seen as opportunities for learning rather than insurmountable obstacles. Regular self-care practices such as adequate sleep, balanced nutrition, and physical activity also contribute to resilience by maintaining overall well-being.

Here are some ways to build resilience:

- Foster a growth mindset by viewing failures as learning experiences.
- Prioritize self-care activities such as getting enough sleep, eating nutritious meals, and engaging in regular exercise.
- Practice self-compassion by treating yourself with the same kindness and understanding you would offer a friend.

Study tips tailored to individual learning styles can enhance preparedness and reduce anxiety. Some students may find visual aids like charts and diagrams helpful, while others might benefit from auditory resources like lectures or podcasts. Identifying and leveraging your learning style enables more efficient study sessions. Additionally, active learning techniques such as teaching the material to someone else or discussing it in study groups can deepen understanding and boost recall.

Emphasizing the importance of psychological resilience in test-taking situations cannot be overstated. Building this resilience involves acknowledging both strengths and weaknesses and seeking support when needed. This might involve talking to a mentor or counselor who can offer guidance and encouragement. Realizing that asking for help is a strength, not a weakness, is pivotal.

To sum up, effectively managing and reducing test anxiety involves a multi-faceted approach grounded in evidence-based strategies. Psychological techniques, breathing exercises, mindfulness practices, and tailored study tips all play significant roles. Emphasizing preparation, emotional regulation, and psychological resilience ensures a holistic strategy that can transform how students handle the pressures of academic assessments. With these tools, the balance between personal responsibility and a supportive safety net can indeed lead to enhanced performance and reduced anxiety.

Reiterating Key Takeaways

Managing and reducing test anxiety can often feel like a daunting task, but it is far from impossible. Cognitive-behavioral approaches and relaxation techniques have been shown through various studies to be highly effective in addressing these issues. The first step in employing cognitive-behavioral strategies involves identifying negative thought patterns that frequently accompany test anxiety. This might include thoughts such as "I'm going to fail" or "I can't do this." Once these thoughts are identified, the next move can be towards challenging them and replacing them with more positive, realistic ones.

- Begin by keeping a journal of your thoughts when you study or prepare for exams. Note the moments when anxious thoughts appear and what triggers them.

- When you identify a negative thought, ask yourself whether it is based on facts or assumptions. Challenge these thoughts by questioning their validity.

- Replace the negative thoughts with positive affirmations. For instance, instead of thinking, "I'm going to fail," you can rephrase it to, "I have prepared well, and I will do my best."

Relaxation techniques are another powerful tool in combating test anxiety. They help calm the mind and body, allowing for better focus and performance. Techniques like deep breathing, progressive muscle relaxation, and guided imagery can be particularly beneficial.

- Practice deep breathing exercises daily. Sit comfortably, close your eyes, and take slow, deep breaths, counting to four as you inhale and six as you exhale.

- Progressive muscle relaxation involves tensing and then slowly relaxing different muscle groups. Start from your toes and work your way up to your head.

- Guided imagery is about visualizing a peaceful and positive scenario. Imagine yourself in a serene place, feeling calm and confident. Use all your senses to make this image as vivid as possible.

Mindfulness practices and principles of positive psychology can significantly enhance one's focus, confidence, and overall well-being during exams. Mindfulness involves staying present in the moment and being aware of one's thoughts and feelings without judgment. This practice can reduce anxiety by preventing ruminative thinking and helping individuals stay grounded.

- Incorporate mindfulness meditation into your daily routine. Spend just ten minutes each day sitting quietly and focusing on your breath.

- During study sessions, practice mindful studying by eliminating distractions and fully engaging with the material at hand.

- Use mindfulness techniques during exams to bring yourself back to the present moment, especially if you find your mind wandering to anxious thoughts.

Positive psychology, on the other hand, emphasizes building strengths and cultivating gratitude. It can play a vital role in boosting exam performance and reducing stress.

- Maintain a gratitude journal where you note down three things you are thankful for every day. This simple act can shift your focus from what's wrong to what's right in your life.

- Engage in activities that boost your mood and confidence, such as hobbies, physical exercise, or spending time with loved ones.

- Surround yourself with positive influences and engage in self-compassion. Remind yourself that it's okay to make mistakes and that they are part of the learning process.

Effective study strategies also form an integral part of managing test anxiety. Procrastination tends to exacerbate anxiety, while organized study schedules can help lessen it. The key is not just to study hard but to study smart.

- Break down your study material into manageable chunks and create a clear study schedule. Set specific goals for each study session.

- Employ active learning techniques such as summarizing information in your own words, teaching the material to someone else, or using flashcards.

- Take regular breaks during study sessions to avoid burnout. The Pomodoro Technique, which involves studying for 25 minutes and then taking a 5-minute break, can be quite effective.

Seeking support is another crucial aspect of overcoming test anxiety and achieving academic success. It is essential to recognize when to reach out for help and to know who to turn to for assistance.

- Forming or joining a study group can provide mutual support and motivation. It also allows for sharing tips and strategies for managing anxiety.

- Seek help from teachers, tutors, or mentors who can provide guidance and clarify doubts. They can also offer strategies tailored to your specific needs.

- If test anxiety becomes overwhelming, consider speaking to a counselor or a mental health professional. They can offer personalized, evidence-based strategies for managing anxiety.

In summary, the journey to managing and reducing test anxiety is multifaceted, involving a combination of cognitive-behavioral strategies, relaxation techniques, mindfulness practices, positive psychology, effective study strategies, and seeking support. By integrating these approaches into your routine, you can enhance your focus, boost your confidence, and improve your overall well-being, ultimately leading to better exam performance. Remember, the goal is not just to excel academically but to maintain a healthy balance between striving for success and nurturing your mental health.

Ending on a High Note

In this chapter, we have explored a variety of strategies designed to manage and reduce test anxiety effectively. We began by discussing cognitive-behavioral techniques that help in transforming negative thought patterns into positive and constructive ones. This approach is integral in creating a mindset that can handle the pressures of exams with greater confidence. Positive affirmations were also highlighted as a means to reinforce self-belief and readiness.

Breathing exercises emerged as practical tools for immediate stress relief. Techniques such as diaphragmatic breathing and the 4-7-8 method offer quick and accessible ways to calm the nervous system during high-pressure moments. These practices contribute significantly to physiological calmness, which in turn supports better focus and performance during exam situations.

Mindfulness practices were emphasized for their role in fostering present-moment awareness. By focusing on the here and now, students can mitigate anxieties related to future outcomes or past experiences. Simple mindfulness exercises, such as observing one's breath, can gradually enhance emotional regulation and mental clarity.

The importance of well-structured preparation cannot be overstated. A strategic study plan, consisting of manageable goals and regular review sessions, was recommended to prevent last-minute panic and reinforce learning. Mock tests and practice exams were suggested to build familiarity with exam formats and assess progress.

Emotional regulation was another key point, with techniques like journaling providing an outlet for anxious thoughts. Recognizing recurring thought patterns through expressive writing can lead to deeper insights and reduced anxiety over time. Additionally, building psychological resilience was discussed as a crucial component. Adopting a growth mindset, prioritizing self-care, and practicing self-compassion were all highlighted as ways to bolster resilience.

Ultimately, these strategies form a multi-faceted approach to managing test anxiety. By integrating cognitive-behavioral techniques, relaxation methods, mindfulness practices, and effective study habits, students can better prepare for exams both mentally and emotionally. The underlying theme is that each student must find what works best for them, tailoring these strategies to suit individual needs and preferences.

It is essential to keep in mind that managing test anxiety is an ongoing process. While these techniques provide valuable tools, persistence and consistency are key. Students should remain open to adapting their strategies and seeking support when necessary. Professional guidance from mentors, teachers, or mental health professionals can provide additional support and personalized strategies.

Reflecting on our initial discussion, it becomes evident that the goal is not merely to achieve academic success but to do so in a manner that maintains overall well-being. Effective management of test anxiety can transform academic experiences, leading to enhanced performance and a more balanced approach to education. As students continually refine their approaches, they cultivate skills that extend beyond the classroom, fostering resilience and adaptability in various aspects of life.